What Makes You Tick

Uniquely You Resources
P. O. Box 490
Blue Ridge, GA 30513

What Makes You Tick

ISBN: 0-9627245-2-1

WHAT MAKES YOU

...And What Ticks You Off!

Mels Carbonell, Ph.D.

Uniquely You Resources
Blue Ridge, GA

Table of Contents

Acknowledgments 1
Foreword 3
Introduction 5

Part 1 — Why people do what they do! **7**
1 What Makes You Tick Is Often What Ticks You Off 9
2 My History is His Story 21
3 So Close, Yet So Far 27
4 Differences That Divide 35
5 The Mystery Of Motivation 41
Part 2 — Understanding Natural Gifts **51**
6 An Ancient Discovery For Modern Times 53
7 Controlling The Dominant Personality 67
8 Calming The Inspiring Personality 81
9 Stimulating The Shy Personality 93
10 Satisfying The Cautious Personality 107
11 Discovering Your Behavioral Blends 123
12 Choices And Changes: Practical Applications 141
Part 3 — Understanding Spiritual Gifts **159**
13 God's Gifts To You..... And Through You 161
14 Combining Personalities With Spiritual Gifts 171
15 Where Do You Fit? 187
Part 4 — Conflict Resolution **203**
16 Handling The Hot Potato Of Conflict 205
17 Biblical Resolution Management 215
18 Are You Enduring Or Enjoying Your Relationships? 225
19 Call For Commitment 239

Appendices **242**
Appendix 1 —Beyond Profiling 243
Appendix 2 —Warnings 251
Appendix 3 —Uniquely You Resources 265

*Dedicated to
my sister,
Algy Edwards
and brother,
Vlic Carbonell,
my heros, and
survivors
in the
struggles of life.*

Acknowledgments

I want to thank Zig Ziglar for encouraging me to take this information and put it into print and cassette form. In my opinion he is the best corporate trainer alive today. I'm honored to have served him.

I want to personally thank Don Sapaugh, former C. E. O. of Rapha Treatment Centers, who published my original book. He believes in me and my message, and his encouragement and support have been instrumental in getting this book published.

Pat Springle, Richard Price, Hal Haller, Jr., and Danny Austin edited and shaped the content of this book. I appreciate their contribution to the clarity and attractiveness of its message.

Above all, I want to thank God for His grace and gift of eternal life. Before coming to know the Lord personally, I failed to see the difference between a religion and a personal relationship with God through Jesus Christ. What a difference that personal relationship with Christ makes!

I've had my fill of humanism and the "human potential" emphasis. Every man-centered philosophy of life will ultimately fail. They never satisfy; they only magnify the emptiness of life. The Old Testament Book of Ecclesiastes communicates a lesson on the futility of life. It proves that life without God is a dead-end street.

I'll never know every why, what, where, and how of life, but I know Who has the answers. We can go beyond understanding why we do what we do; in fact, we can know the One who created us. Then, we genuinely begin to find our true identities.

Foreword

Several years ago I sat at breakfast with someone who really caused me to think. It was early in the morning, but what he said made me wide awake. His comments puzzled me at first, but I soon saw what he meant. He said, "Zig, did you know you can't motivate anyone?" Keep in mind, I make a living motivating people. And here's someone telling me I can't motivate anyone. I asked, "What do you mean by that?"

He explained that all motivation is intrinsic — that people do what they do for their own reasons, not anyone else's. We can intimidate or manipulate (which is wrong), but we cannot motivate others. This really got to me and I questioned, "Well, what do you call what I do?" I surely didn't feel like I ever intimidated or manipulated anyone. So, what in the world was he driving at?

He quickly responded, "Zig, you're a master climate creator and environment engineer. You create the climate and environment that makes people self-motivated — to do what they ought to do; not because you made them do it, but because they decided on their own."

I smiled and he sighed. I then invited him to do training for me in Dallas. That was my first encounter with Dr. Mels Carbonell. He made me think and I appreciated it. He was also gracious enough to explain what he meant without sounding superior.

His training in Dallas was great. It helped me understand more about being personality wise. The concepts he presented, which are all in this notebook, are not new, just fresh. They are not way-out, but down-home. The truths you'll read are simple, yet profound . . . scientific, yet practical.

As I travel throughout the country speaking on management, sales training and motivation, I consistently notice a single thread that weaves in and out of each meeting. A question that clamors for an answer. How to be people smart . . . how to manage people better . . . how to be people effective.

How to be personality wise says it best. This book answers those questions and more.

Zig Ziglar
Best-selling author and expert on motivation
Dallas, Texas

Introduction

I was raised in an unbelieving home and never went to church until I was in junior high school. My father was once very religious, but he got turned off to "religianity" because of turmoil in the church. When I was a small child, I remember him telling me, "the church was full of hypocrites. All they ever do is fight each other!" My first impression about churches was confusing. They were supposed to teach love and peace, but they seemed full of conflict and division.

I finally realized Jesus was the issue, not what Christians or churches did. What Christ did (and does), not what I or others do, is most important. Jesus was never socially unjust, racially discriminate, or hypocritical. I had to decide if He was what He claimed to be and did what He claimed to do.

After a time of intense study and soul-searching, I concluded Jesus was truly divine. He lived, died and rose again to pay for my guilt. He bought my pardon on Calvary. He offered eternal life to all who simply trust Him. He also established His church to help Christians grow and mature. The plan is perfect, but people aren't.

Ironically, I learned that my father was partially right. Churches are full of conflicts, but Christ is still the same — yesterday, today and tomorrow. Though people cause trouble in churches, Christ is still the problem-solver.

I love the Lord with all my heart. I believe His church is still alive. The home and the church are God-ordained institutions. I love my church, my pastor, my brothers and sisters in Christ. I've been a Christian for over thirty years, and I speak in all kinds of churches nationwide nearly every week. The problem I see is this: Christians have the incredible resources of God's love, God's wisdom, and God's power, but most of them don't know how to avoid and resolve conflicts. We can establish great programs to reach the lost, disciple Christians, feed the poor, and construct huge buildings. We can pray for millions of dollars for missions, pray demons out of the possessed, heal the sick, and even change the law of the land. We seem powerless, however, when it comes to avoiding and resolving conflicts.

For many years I have surveyed and profiled churches and pastors concerning their personalities and conflicts in ministry. Few churches have resources to help their members deal with conflicts. Pastors seem more concerned about networking, involvement, and assimilation than team building and togetherness. In my opinion, however, unity is more important than finding a place in ministry.

This book is designed to help Christians identify their motivations in relationship to others — how we relate to those who irritate! We must learn how to live peaceably with those who offend us. Understanding human behavior from a biblical perspective is the key to resolving conflicts and genuinely loving one another.

As you read these pages, I hope you will understand yourself more fully. You will also understand others and especially God better. These insights will help you avoid and resolve conflicts. And God will be glorified!

Part 1

Why people do what they do!

1

What Makes You Tick Is Often What Ticks You Off

Just because you're a Christian doesn't mean you understand what makes you tick. In the eyes of many people, I was a successful pastor of a growing church before I began to understand myself. My church had just been recognized as "Florida's fastest growing church." We started with 49 people and had nearly 1500 attend a year later. According to Dr. Elmer Towns and Christian Life Magazine, we experienced "America's largest first anniversary for a church in history"!

I was flying higher than a kite, but sometimes I felt lower than a skunk. Some people said I was dictatorial. Others condemned me for "building my own kingdom." I knew my heart, and didn't feel they were right. I loved the Lord. I simply wanted people to know Christ and make Him known. It was an exciting—but confusing—time for me.

My journey toward discovery began when I attended a course at Dallas Theological Seminary. At a workshop on two assessment tools, the Taylor-Johnson Temperament Assessment and the

Performax (or DISC), I received my first hint about my true motivations and personality. I had always been an aggressive achiever. I was assertive and sure of myself. As a new Christian, I had asked God to make me quiet and passive, but the more I grew in the Word, the "worse" I seemed to get. I became even more vocal and outgoing, and I wanted to tell everybody about Jesus. I couldn't understand why everyone wasn't more excited about the Lord!

At this workshop, I was introduced to the DISC assessment. It was enlightening. This assessment revealed my natural motivations, and I learned what made me tick and what ticked me off. For the first time in my life, I understood how and why God made my particular personality.

Since then, I have observed the entire spectrum of relationships and conflicts with people, especially in church. We desperately need to learn how to deal with our differences. We battle over backgrounds, presumptions, expectations, communication, and personalities. We constantly struggle and wonder why. No question is more practical than: "Why do we have so many problems with people?" The Book of James, the "Proverbs of the New Testament," asks the same question in chapter 4 verse 1: "Where do fights and quarrels come from?" James then answers by giving the insight that our problems come from our misperceptions and twisted motivations: "Don't they come from within ourselves — from our desires and actions that war within us?"

Understanding "what makes us tick" is central to understanding why we have problems with people. Misunderstandings lead to clashes, and these conflicts hinder our effectiveness as mates, parents, and Christians. The word discord illustrates it best. The prefix *dis* means "separation, negation, or reversal." *Cord* denotes the element that binds people or things together. Discord, therefore, is anything that divides and destroys relationships. The tie that binds can become the knots in our stomachs! The things that often bring us together can also drive us apart. We need to recognize our motivations and behaviors in order to learn how to avoid and resolve conflicts.

Understanding Our Motivations

Solving our people problems involves understanding our motivations, and the science of human behavior can help explain these motivations. Varied behavior makes studying personality types a fascinating exercise. There is nothing more intriguing than discovering an individual's motivation. Daily human drama revolves around the reasons for and results of our actions. Unlocking the mystery of motivation and behavior is the key to understanding people.

Comprehending personalities is what the science of human behavior is all about. In order to live, work, and play in a healthy and happy environment, we need to understand why people do what they do. Being able to "read" people makes life exciting and enjoyable, yet people are often the cause of life's biggest problems. Perhaps you've heard or said, "Life would be great if it weren't for people!" It's a humorous but sad commentary on how we view one another.

It is helpful to analyze our motives from a biblical perspective as well as from a scientific, empirical perspective. The science of human behavior and the Scriptures harmonize as they reveal our motives. God speaks through His Word and through the world around us. He teaches us how to believe and behave. There is no contradiction between true science and the Scriptures, between the secular and the sacred. Truth is truth wherever you find it.

Natural and Spiritual Gifts

When Christians speak of "giftedness," most of them are referring to spiritual gifts, such as showing mercy, pastor / shepherd, teaching, and exhortation. I believe, however, there are two kinds of gifts God bestows: natural gifts and spiritual gifts. Spiritual gifts are given to believers at the point of their conversion to Christ; natural gifts — our personalities — are granted to each person at the point of conception and developed during the earliest years of life. Recent studies of sextuplets show that approximately 35% of a person's personality is genetically based, that is, about a third of what makes us tick is engineered in our DNA. Another 50% of a person's personality is shaped by childhood development up to the age of 6. The nurturing and protection of parents during this period dramatically affects — for good or ill — the person's motivations and behaviors for the rest of his or her life. The remaining part of a personality development comes from experiences throughout the rest of childhood and adolescence.

Our personalities, then, are gifts of God which are engineered genetically and shaped by our childhood experiences Every human being has been endowed by God with a pattern of motivations, desires, and responses. We are all "made in the image of God" with will, intellect, and emotions. That image is tarnished by sin, but a remnant remains. Spiritual gifts, however, are only bestowed on those who trust Christ as their Savior. Their purpose is to enable each believer to play a specific, effective role in the dynamic ministry of the body of Christ. We will examine spiritual gifts later in the book. For now, let's focus on our natural gifts, the personality God has given each of us.

Observing Human Behavior

Self-evaluation can be helpful, or it can be dangerous. We must be honest with ourselves and God, but objective evaluation of our hidden motives and behaviors can be a frightening experience.

Knowing who we are is not as important as Whose we are. We belong to God, not only because He made us, but also because He bought us through the ultimate payment of Christ's death on the cross. Our comprehension of the cross purifies our purposes and energizes our motivations. In his book, *The Cross of Christ*, John R. W. Stott writes:

> ". . . it would be most unseemly to feign cool detachment as we contemplate Christ's cross. For willy-nilly we are involved. Our sins put him there. So, far from offering us flattery, the cross undermines our self righteousness. We can stand before it only with a bowed head and a broken spirit. And there we remain until the Lord Jesus speaks to our hearts his word of pardon and acceptance, and we, gripped by his love and brimful of thanksgiving, go out into the world to live our lives in his service."

Being honest about our behavior begins with understanding the truth about ourselves. Once we begin to identify our strengths and weaknesses, we can understand God's plan in our relationships and behavior.

Human behavior science focuses on the emotions and behaviors of normal people. Basically, psychologists and psychiatrists try to help the 10% of people who exhibit self destructive behavior due to severe emotional trauma, a chemical imbalance, rebellion, or some other compelling reason in the person's life. Human behavior scientists explain the reasons and actions of the other 90% of people who do what they do because of natural and normal reasons. However, this doesn't mean normal people don't occasionally do abnormal things. Everyone is capable of abnormal behavior, but what most normal people do can be explained by understanding their personalities. Most of our problems would be avoided and/or solved, if we simply recognized the truth of how our actions affect us and others.

On the other hand, abnormal people often do what they do because of deeper drives and compulsions. This book is intended to help people with normal emotional challenges. Those with abnormal behavior are encouraged to see qualified professionals who can help them. Christ said, "They that are sick need a physician" (Luke 5:31).

Everyone Has Problems

Even though most people could use good Christian counseling, everyone needs to learn more about the Word of God and how it applies to our everyday problems. We need to know how to especially improve our living endorsements of "the greatest story ever told!"

The Bible is the greatest resource to help us learn how to work, live, and worship with others. Its pages give insights about our challenges with people . . . especially ourselves! Though the Bible is obviously our best source to solve our problems, ironically, authors today have capitalized on biblical truth without giving God the credit. Many books are published each year full of "truth" without any reference to God or the Bible.

There are numerous passages of Scriptures dealing with relationships and conflict resolution. Scores of seminars and courses—both Christian and secular—are offered every day to help people deal with their conflicts. Much of the information taught is simple, ancient truth with modern terminology. We must equip ourselves with the necessary information in order to make solid judgments about the future in our relationships with others.

Knowing how to deal with people according to their temperaments and drives is paramount in relationships of all types, not just business management relationships. Understanding personalities is vital to surviving in the work world; and we cannot overestimate its importance in avoiding bad marriages and family frustrations.

Because divisions and disharmony are a fact of life, we need more than religious platitudes and "grin and bear it" attitudes to help us deal with these sticky situations.

The science of motivation focuses on the reasons we feel and respond the way we do. Just as the science of biology reveals the classifications of biological life—genera, species, phyla, and kingdoms—so the science of human behavior reveals there are classifications of behaviors. There are also hundreds of different elements in chemistry. Each one is different, but they are all part of the Periodic Table. There are many different cloud formations in meteorology. All scientific classifications represent predictable responses to various situations,and in human behavior science, there are identifiable, predictable personalities types.

Truth That Is Not In The Bible

Someone once asked me why the Four Temperament Model is not found in the Bible. My response is because the Bible is not a science book. The Four Temperament Model is a scientific method of viewing human behavior. The Bible is a book of theology, not anthropology or biology, therefore it does not contain all the facts of science.

When the Bible touches scientific subjects, it is accurate. Everything in the Bible is true, but all truth is not in the Bible. All the books in the world could not contain all the truth there is. For instance, you will not find the mathematical tables in the Bible, but that does not mean the mathematical tables aren't true. There are many more truths in nature which someday will be discovered. These truths will not contradict the Bible, and they are just as true as if they were written in the Bible because they are a part of God's natural, or general, revelation. We make a grave mistake when we reject truth just because it is not found in the Bible. The Dark Ages were characterized by people who rejected scientific discovery just because it was not found in the Scriptures. In that day, people refused to believe the truths of science because there were no biblical references to support the science. Throughout history, godly individuals who believed God gave truth in science as well as in the Scriptures have suffered persecution from sincere yet ignorant believers.

Motivation

There is a myth about the science of motivation. That myth is: "We can motivate others." Coaches give stimulating pep talks to inspire the team to win the game. Teachers may try to persuade students to do better by scolding them. Parents may restrict their children's freedom, hoping to force them to improve their grades. These tactics may motivate some, but not most.

The truth is that we can't motivate anyone to do anything he doesn't want to do. People do what they do because of their own reasons, not ours. We can try to manipulate and intimidate (which are wrong), but we can't motivate them. Manipulation and intimidation often backfire. Using outside force to get people to do things can boomerang to hurt and haunt us. All true motivation is intrinsic; it comes from within. People are motivated by their own feelings and for their own reasons.

Have you ever said, "I wish my child was motivated!" or "If that person was only motivated to . . . !" Everyone is motivated, whether they take the particular action we want them to take or not. Some children are motivated to study; others are motivated not to study. The decision to act or not act is driven by the will of the individual. It is incorrect to say some people are not motivated because they don't take a particular action.

Motivation is not the ability to scream until people give in and do what we want. It's not a pep talk just before the game. Motivation takes root and becomes personalized before we ever go into action.

It begins with our personalities, that is, why we do what we do. The key is creating the climate and environment which make people want to do what they should do. (See Chapter 5 for more insights on motivation.)

There Are No Bad Personalities

Comprehending the dynamic differences in personalities will profoundly affect our lives. Our personalities are the unique ways we think, feel and act: the ways God "wired" us to respond. No personality is better than the others.

Someone is probably thinking: "But you haven't met my mother-in-law!" or "You don't know my boss!" Perhaps these people are terrors. However, it's not a rotten personality, but rather how they use their personalities which makes them behave so poorly. I don't believe anyone has a bad personality. I believe we receive the germ of our personalities from God at conception. He made each of us distinct and different for a purpose.

Many (if not most) of our conflicts arise because we don't understand each other. Fear, awe, mockery, and envy result because of our differences. What one person sees as good, another may see as bad. The Bible tells us "all good gifts come from above" (James 1:17). The Psalmist penned, "It is He who has made us, not we ourselves" (Psalm 100:3). God "wired" everyone with unique personalities, and their parents and experiences also influenced and shaped them. The exciting reality is that God is not finished with us. He continues to work, conforming us into the image of Christ (Romans 8:29).

The way we were raised (the environment of our early childhood) has much to do with the development of our personalities. Nature and nurture both mold us into who and what we are. Because of Adam and Eve's disobedience, all humankind is cursed with a sin nature. We're depraved, but God has also given us a conscience to help us know right from wrong. He has given us dignity. We have been created in God's image, so as Christians, we have both dignity and a God-given identity because we are His children. We were "delivered from the domain of darkness and transferred into the kingdom of His beloved Son" (Col 1:13).

Although the way we feel and think has definitely been influenced by our past, it does not have to control us. We have a choice: We can allow our personalities to control us or we can control our personalities. Better yet, we can allow the Holy Spirit to master our temperaments, to temper and strengthen us for God's glory.

Keep in mind, we are discussing the emotions of normal people. We are not looking at abnormal behavior—self destructive patterns of behavior which may be the result of abuse, abandonment, disease, chemical imbalance, or rebellion. Everyone experiences the range of simple to serious conflicts with others. By understanding predictable patterns of behavior, we can avoid some of these clashes, and we can learn to resolve others. We become more tolerant of differing personalities as we gain insight into the motivations of others by simply recognizing the normal drives and passions of people.

Relationships

Someone said, "Most relationships don't end due to sudden blowouts, but instead, from slow leaks." Those slow leaks of misunderstandings, misreadings, and misgivings destroy our relationships. It's the little foxes that spoil the vine (Song of Solomon 2:15).

I remember a couple who were once very much in love. They were the perfect picture of love, but early in the relationship, the husband began to tease his wife about a small weakness. At first she laughed at his pointed puns, but his teasing turned to fault-finding, and her laughter turned to tears. Like a nail in a tire, her feelings were pierced. A little leak developed in their relationship. He became more irritated with her problem, and she became more self-conscious. She needed help, but he rode her wounded spirit until their relationship became flat. There was no understanding or tolerance, just annoyance and pressure. Eventually her love, like a tire low on air and over heating from the friction of criticism, blew out. What began as a beautiful journey ended in a fatal crash of heartache, despair, and estrangement.

Our personalities are simply instruments in the hands of God. God never intended us to use our personalities as excuses to do wrong. Instead, God expects us to control our personalities to glorify Him.

ENDNOTES

[1]Stott, John, R.W., *The Cross of Christ*, (Downers Grove: Intervarsity Press, 1986), p. 11.

2

My History Is His Story

I was raised an atheist. My father came from Cuba to the United States in 1928. He was very religious and even studied for the priesthood. I remember him telling me the story of how he walked to work, "six miles in the snow every day in New York" and prayed through his Rosary beads along the way. He was committed to his church, but something happened. He became disillusioned with religion. He first became an agnostic, then an atheist, and eventually a communist.

In the early 1950's he was arrested and tried by Senator Joseph McCarthy's committee in the hearings on un-American activities. His picture was on the front page of the *Miami Herald*. He was on the television evening news. It was so exciting to me! I thought of him as a celebrity. I was in elementary school and a little naive. I wasn't as embarrassed as I should have been. I simply looked at my father's problem as a political thing. "And besides," I thought, "this is America with freedom of speech, religion, and political preference."

This was the beginning of my so-called "dysfunctional" development. Actually, it didn't affect me as much as my sister who is 10 years older than I. She was working for an attorney at the time, and she was fired from her job because of our father's notoriety. In spite of her difficulties, she has become a stable and successful person. She is a master-teacher who just retired from the Bibb County School Board. She was also voted "Spanish Teacher Of The Year" in the State of Georgia.

If anyone in our family has an excuse for poor behavior, my sister does. But I'm proud to say, she's almost perfect by my standards! Of course, I'm her little brother and she's my faultless big sister. She's obviously not perfect, but here's another case of someone who really went through the mill and came out well-adjusted.

We were not only raised atheists and communists, but our dad was also a spy for the Castro government. He must not have been a very good spy. . . because we were always poor! (I want to believe he was a good spy but gave whatever financial gain he earned away.) He was an idealist. Wealth and possessions were not important to him, therefore we often went without. But we didn't seem to care because we were loved. Our mother was a saint to have endured all this communist subterfuge and confusion. She was the stabilizing one in the family. Her faithfulness and strength endured the pain and protected us from more than we could bear.

Looking back, I now realize all this could have been a reason to go off the edge, but instead, I recognize God is sovereign and allows bad things to happen to people for a reason. Sometimes He allows a crooked stick to point a straight path. My past is obviously twisted and tangled with intrigue, but my present and future are full of hope and joy. I've learned the past doesn't have to control the future. We can live above our history of problems.

All Of History Is Really His Story

I like to think of our personal history as "His story" — Christ's story in our lives. Everyone has a history, but it's "His story" in us that really matters. God's amazing grace and everything that touches our lives are all part of His permissive and prescriptive will. He allows these things to mold and make us into better people. He gives us new experiences and opportunities to share "His story" and show His love and strength to others.

For over forty years I have not been able to share "the rest of the story," but now I can. For those of you who are trying to figure out the real reason why I never shared it, it's simply because my father asked me not to. He just passed away at 91 years of age. My sister, brother, and I have decided to share our story now in hope that it will help us and others deal with the past.

The dark and hidden side to my past didn't make me into a twisted and troubled individual. My dad was an atheist, communist, and spy, but he gave each of us fascinating names. My dad was very creative. We each have four letter acronyms in our first names. My sister's name is Algy. It was originally Algi, but my dad changed it to Algy when she came to America, probably because it looked too much like seaweed! In Spanish, it stands for "forward with the international war."

My brother's name is Vlic. By the way, he has also turned out quite well. He's six years older than I and had a tremendous influence on my determination and tenacious motivations. His name stands for "long live international communism."

Marx, Engels, Lenin, & Stalin

My name is the most spectacular. (At least, that's what I think.) I've spent over 40 years keeping it to myself, and I now want everyone to say "Wow!" when I tell them that my name, Mels, stands for "Marx, Engels, Lenin, and Stalin."

Many people ask, "Who was Engels?" He was Marx' money man. He financed the Communist Revolution. It's odd how Marx used a capitalist to support his revolution against capitalism. Communism is full of strange paradoxes.

Stranger still is how God took a little communist's kid, confronted me with the Good News of the gospel, and revolutionized me into a Christian. I didn't search for religion out of rebellion. I loved and respected my father very much. He was committed to communism, just like I am committed to Christ. He did nothing out of the ordinary in my past to make me turn away from him and his cause. I simply studied communism and Christianity, and Christianity made a whole lot more sense.

I concluded communism can't work with "fallen" human beings. Communism is based on people being satisfied with equality, but if we're all selfish sinners in need of a Savior, communism will not work. Actually, the early church practiced a form of socialism in which everyone was equal and shared their possessions with others in need. But communism and the purest of ideals cannot survive in a sin-cursed world with selfish people in control. Only with Christ as ruler in our lives will we ever be able to experience true communal care and common love for one another.

While I was comfortable with agnosticism as a young teenager, I was confronted with the truth of Christianity. Ironically, it was also science that actually lead me to Christ. I was convinced the Bible and science did not agree, and that the Bible was full of fables and fairy tales. My answer to everything was evolution. My dad had taught me well.

But God brought a teenage friend and little church in my life. My friend, Buddy Tickle, invited me to a youth meeting where the gospel was presented clearly. I also received a tract challenging me to find one scientific error in the Bible. It offered a $1000 reward. Dr. Harry Rimmer of the Research Science Bureau offered this reward for many years without any takers.

I was convinced I could find several "fantasies" in the Bible and claim my $1000. At the same time, I was given a book, *The Bible And Modern Science*, authored by Dr. Henry Morris, Dean of the Civil Engineering Department at Virginia Polytechnical Institute. God used this book, my friend Buddy, and many other people to convince me the Bible is the trustworthy, inspired, infallible Word of God.

God Bless The Gideons

The first Bible I ever saw was on my Kensington Park Elementary School teacher's desk. My first Bible was actually a Gideon Bible my brother "borrowed" from a motel while on a football trip in Orlando.

I used that Gideon Bible to try and disprove it in order to claim my $1000 reward. The more I studied, the more I discovered the Bible had scientific facts recorded before man ever discovered them, such as: the earth is round, the stars are innumerable, light can be parted, the earth is suspended in space by nothing, air has weight — scientific fact after scientific fact. I concluded the Bible was a supernatural book inspired by a supernatural author, God.

I reasoned it would take more faith *not* to believe the Bible than to believe it. I came to this conclusion because of the facts and evidences of Scripture, not because of what my parents told me. The Bible made sense, so trust in its author was the logical step to take.

My journey is unique, but so is everyone else's, even those who were saved "while living in deep sin at the age of 5, addicted to drugs (Flintstone vitamins!) and strung out on pacifiers." You may think your past is boring and dull, but I would give almost everything to have had that experience. When I was growing up, I never had my parents read me a Bible story, or my dad to tell me about Jesus, or my mother to pray with me, or say grace at the dinner table, or go to church as a family.

Perhaps you don't have a "gutter to glory" testimony. Perhaps your history is not that spectacular, but you do have His story to show and tell. Regardless what has happened to you in the past, your future is as bright as the promises of God.

Learn to live victoriously, above all your past or present problems. Live with eternity's values in view. His story is also your story, if you have trusted Christ as your Savior and allowed Him to be the Lord of your feelings, thoughts, and actions.

3

So Close, Yet So Far

We're alike . . . yet so different! My wife and I share many interests and values, yet we're different in many ways. She is a very organized, clean, and neat person. I try to be neat, but compared to my wife, I'm a slob! Once I was recognized in college for having the most pants and shirts on one door knob. I had 18 pairs of pants and shirts hanging on one knob. At least I hung them up!

Soon after we were married, I got up in the middle of the night to go to the bathroom, and when I returned, my side of the bed was already made! You know that story isn't true, but perhaps you have gone to get the mail or taken out the garbage, only to return and find the door locked! You may have gotten upset and sighed, "Why did you lock the door? I just went to get the mail."

Your mate may have responded, "You can't be too safe nowadays. It's just as easy for you to take your key as it is for me to worry about the door being unlocked." That sounds logical . . . to your mate!

Hopefully, your mate is committed to Christ and to permanency in marriage. You don't worry about divorce, but you must confess humorously, you have worried about being murdered! Some people could literally drive others crazy. Commitment, not compatibility, is most important, but understanding our potential incompatibility is vital to working through conflicts. People are different in many ways, but those differences are most apparent in their behavior. While some people remain cool, calm, and collected, others are excitable, enthusiastic, and explosive. Some are very passive and others very active, but we should not conclude that one is "good" and the other "bad." Each individual responds uniquely, and those responses are predictable.

Differences

God designed us so we need each other, and He gave us different personalities so we could relate and respond to people better. No one is completely self sufficient. In other words, we are not complete without Christ and others. Some people are predominantly active, while others are usually passive. "Fight or flight" differences are evident, but again, one is not better than the other. God designed these differences in our personalities to make us appreciate—and need—others. Without the differences, we would become self sufficient and lonely.

Your personality may cause you to withdraw or aggressively prove yourself. Some of us avoid conflict at all cost; some of us relish it! The apostle Paul was aggressive, but the disciple Thomas was cautious. Peter enjoyed being up front, but his brother, Andrew, was often behind the scenes.

You seldom find a Marine drill sergeant sheepishly leading with a sweet, soft voice. A gentle personality doesn't fit that job. But also, you seldom see the rough and tough type who eats nails for breakfast working as a kindergarten teacher. There are exceptions to the rule, but they are rare. People seem to fit in roles where they feel most comfortable and confident. For example, in John 11:20 Martha is obviously the more active one, while Mary is more cautious and reflective. The Bible does not judge the response of either sister as better or worse. It simply characterizes the two different behaviors.

We tend to gravitate toward roles which fit our personalities, and we struggle in roles where our temperaments are tested. People have comfort zones where they are most confident in what they do. Some people challenge the outer limits, but others don't like anyone to threaten their boundaries. Our comfort zones are set by the parameters of our personalities. In other words, life is easier when our personalities are not stretched beyond their limits.

People who withdraw and don't get involved as fast as others are passive. This does not mean they don't care about what's happening. It simply means they initially hold back. Mary cared just as much as Martha, but her response was to wait when she heard Jesus was coming. Passive people can be as capable and caring as active people, but they often wait before responding. They aren't as impulsive as active people.

When Our Personalities Betray Us

As an aggressive and optimistic person, I often find myself wanting to get involved in exciting opportunities. When I pastored, I constantly tried new ways to stimulate growth. I couldn't stand the status quo! Things had to be "growing and going" to glorify God. But I also learned there was a place to be still and know God better. I remember one day in my office. I was all alone . . . except for the Holy Comforter and Discomforter. I faced some staggering problems. I felt so discouraged. I felt weak and vulnerable. I found myself uncharacteristically sensitive and still, and I began to cry. I pulled a book off my shelf and began to read the first chapter on

"Brokenness."

God was in the process of breaking me to use me for His glory. I had been so full of myself, not even God could fill me! I had been so sure and strong, it got me into all sorts of trouble. I needed to be careful of my own personality.

We are most likely to misuse our strengths and abuse our best qualities when we are under stress. At these times, our personalities can suddenly become our worst enemies. Often people wish they had not responded to situations the way they did. Some regret their explosions; others regret their silence. We learn to adapt and respond according to each situation. The most effective people understand why they do what they do. There are times for enthusiastic, active behavior and times for calm, passive responses. Those people who learn the balance prosper most often in their relationships and activities.

Some people believe there is never a place for passive-pessimistic behavior. I was conducting a training seminar when a gentleman challenged me, "I don't believe in being negative about anything for any reason. It's never good to be negative!"

I responded with the simple question, "Was that a positive or negative statement?"

He thought for only a second or two, then he came right back with, "I'm positively against anything negative!" That's really going too far with Positive Mental Attitude!

Keep in mind, most of the Ten Commandments begin with "Thou shalt NOT!" All types of behavior—even cautious, reflective behavior—are necessary for balance. To illustrate the need for passive-pessimism, let's pretend that we have just completed a positive mental attitude course. We are preparing to walk along a foot wide cliff, 1,000 feet above the ground, with no handrail. Our leader begins our journey by saying, "Follow me! Hurry now! Isn't this exciting?" It would be difficult to follow a leader who appears so carefree—and careless! In this situation we want a leader who is confident, yet cautious. We expect the leader of this expedition to say, "Now be very cautious. Watch your step. This is dangerous. I don't want anyone to get hurt."

There is a place for passive-pessimistic feelings and actions. Some of life's situations (such as buying a used car) demand a cautious, rational approach which could be labeled passive-pessimistic. Unfortunately, there are some people who remain so passive they never get anything done. They wait and worry rather than do anything. These people could probably benefit from more active, optimistic approach to life's challenges.

There's also a place for active-optimistic behavior. When someone yells, "Fire!" it isn't wise to just sit there and say, "I don't smell anything burning, and I don't see any flames. I'm not moving." You ought to become active and find out what's really happening.

Both active-optimistic and passive-pessimistic behaviors are appropriate in their time and place. Neither is exclusively right nor wrong. Usually we aren't strictly one or the other, but a combination of both. We need to learn to use each approach instead of merely reacting in the way we habitually react. The Bible teaches both types of behavior are appropriate. Matthew 28:19 tells us to "Go into all the world and preach the gospel," a clear call for active behavior. Psalm 46:10 encourages a different response: "Be still and know that I am God." Problems occur because our behavior may be reactionary instead of carefully chosen. One comes easily; the other does not. The solution is being controlled by the Holy Spirit to do what God wants us to do, not what we naturally want to do.

Me-ism Exposed

Someone said, "We need to find ourselves." Well, I found myself and I didn't like what I found! I'm too impulsive and reactive.

It gets me into trouble. I'm too positive and outgoing. I need to let God conform me into what He wants me to be.

God doesn't want us to use our extremes as defenses. God wants us to be able to choose our response to a given situation based on the wisdom He gives for that particular moment. Both passive and active behavior can be good or bad, right or wrong. We must be optimistic about His promises and pessimistic about the world's false hope; positive about good and negative about evil. The church is full of all types of people — those who are active and/or passive; optimistic and/or pessimistic; and positive and/or negative.

There is the group that says, "We need to do something—to get the job done for God." Another group feels, "We need to slow down and get our act together—to commune more with God." Both attitudes are right. Like someone said, "We need to work as though everything depends upon us, but pray as though everything depends upon God." One attitude is active-oriented, while the other is passive-oriented. Active type people in the church need to be more tolerant of the passive people, while the passive people need to be more understanding of the active types. "Bear ye one another's burden" (Galatians 6:2) takes on a whole new perspective in light of our personality differences.

Romans 15:1 commands, "We who are strong ought to bear the infirmities of the weak, and not please ourselves." We can bear the shortcomings of those who cannot control themselves. The stronger believers must bear the burdens of those who are weak in the faith. Most Christians, however, do what they do because of natural impulses rather than spiritual principles.

Conflicts bring out our tendencies to be extroverts or introverts. Active people are more open and aggressive in conflict. Passive people are more closed. They keep it more to themselves or to a small group of people. They tend to be more withdrawn and realistic. If the individual is task-oriented, he will argue over form and function. If the individual is people-oriented, she will debate over feelings and fellowship. One tends to be more "high tech" while the other is more "high touch."

Even people with similar personalities can have conflicts. Two outgoing types can argue over which way to go. Two reserved types may debate over whether to go or not! Conflicts are normal and inevitable, but how we avoid and resolve them must be biblical. Conflicts can hurt us deeply, yet God can use them to shape and mold us for his purposes. Noted author and speaker, J. I. Packer,[1] wrote about the purpose of trials in his outstanding book, Knowing God:

> . . . children know that holiness is their Father's will for them, and that is both a means, condition, and constituent of their happiness, here and hereafter; and because they love their Father they actively seek the fulfilling of His beneficent purpose. Paternal discipline exercised through outward pressures and trials helps the process along: the Christian up to his eyes in trouble can take comfort from the knowledge that in God's kindly plan it all has a positive purpose, to further his sanctification. In this world, royal children have to undergo extra training and discipline, which other children escape, in order to fit them for their high destiny. It is the same with the children of the King of Kings. The clue to understanding all His dealings with them is to remember that throughout their lives He is training them for what awaits them, and chiselling them into the image of Christ. Sometimes the chiselling process is painful, and the discipline irksome; but the Scripture reminds us—'Whom the Lord loveth he chasteneth, and scourgeth every son whom he receiveth. If ye endure chastening, God dealeth with you as with sons . . . Now no chastening for the present seemeth to be joyous, but grievous; nevertheless afterward it yieldeth the peaceable fruit of righteousness . . .'

(Hebrews 12:6f, 11). Only the man who has grasped this can make sense of Romans 8:28, 'All things work together for good to them that love God.'[1]

Even in our difficulties, God has His purposes to produce character and depth in us.

ENDNOTES

[1]Packer, J. I., *Knowing God*, (Downers Grove, IL: InterVarsity Press, 1973), p. 201.

4

Differences That Divide

People are different. That may seem like an obvious, simplis-tic statement, but our grasp of this fact has dramatic consequences in our relationships. In the simplest delineation of the differences in people, we observe that some are motivated by accomplishing tasks and some are motivated by relationships. To illustrate this, let's say a task-oriented person and a people-oriented person are both working in a garden. Someone walks up and says, "Hi, how are you? What's happening?" The task person predictably responds: "I'm busy," or "Come back later." He is so concerned about getting the job done that he doesn't want to talk.

In contrast, the relationally motivated person might respond: "Good to see you! Time for a break. Let's talk." She doesn't care nearly as much about getting the garden done as enjoying relation-ships.

I have a friend who's wife is usually passive in her task-orientation, but he's very active. On their first vacation, they decided to visit Gatlinburg, Tennessee. Before leaving, his wife's first question was, "Do you have a map?"

He replied, "I don't need a map, honey. I've been there before."

She responded, "How far are we going to drive each day?"

"I don't know. Until we get tired, he sighed."

She persisted, "Where are we going to spend the night?"

He was getting tired of the third degree, and he moaned, "There are hundreds of motels all along I-75!"

His wife wasn't through asking questions. "How much money will we need for food and lodging?"

Finally he exploded, "I don't know! And I don't even want to go any more!" Totally frustrated, he complained, "Why do you ask me all these questions?"

His wife likes to plan and prepare. He likes risks and adventures.

Mary and Martha are perfect examples of task- and people-oriented individuals. In Luke 10:40-41, Martha is task-oriented, while Mary focuses on people. In this familiar passage, Mary sits and listens to Jesus while Martha busily prepares dinner.

We can apply these two personality types to the work environment. Imagine a boss telling two workers (one task- and the other people-oriented) the project must be completed by 5:00 or they will be fired. Task-oriented people refuse to be interrupted, and they work until the tasks are accomplished. But relationally oriented people have to control their natural drive to talk when they are interrupted. The wise response is, "I'm sorry I can't talk now. I've got to finish. Let's get together later."

Too Busy

The task person has to learn how to become more people-oriented, and the people person must learn how to be more task-oriented. The key is balance. The challenges of life will make both behaviors necessary.

Martha served busily and faithfully (Luke 10:40), but Mary was interested in being near Jesus. Jesus reproved Martha for being too busy and neglecting the more important activity of sitting and listening. In this case, it seems Martha was wrong and Mary was right because it is more important to be near Jesus than to serve Him. However, even here we need to be careful to be balanced. We all know people who claim to be spiritual but do little that is worthwhile for God. If our worship does not translate into productive work, there is something wrong with our worship. At the same time, we can work for Jesus and never get closer to Him. I like to tell people, "Remember whom you serve, not what you serve." It is more important to know Him better than to serve Him better.

Another way of describing these differences is "high tech" and "high touch." One is concerned with process and thinking. The other cares for people and friendships. A high tech person values form and function, the how to's. High touch people value feelings, caring, and sharing. High tech is interested in things; high touch is concerned about people.

I'm a high touch/active person with my head in the clouds. My wife is high tech/passive. She is usually right about things. I once questioned her, "Are you ever wrong?"

She replied, "Yes, I was wrong once, but then I thought about it, and I realized that I was wrong about that!"

She's the best thing that ever happened to me. She's also my best friend. God gave her to me to complete me. Our personalities clash, but God knows she's exactly what I need.

High tech people are concerned about details; high touch people are interested in relationships. Both are important to society. Can you imagine the world full of one or the other? If there were only high tech people, a lot would be accomplished but with little compassion for others. If there were only high touch people, little would be accomplished, and eventually, people would get very frustrated. With all of the high tech advancements today, we must be careful not to lose our high touch abilities. Technology is advancing, but relationships are falling apart. The computer has caused an accelerated growth in the sciences, the least of which is human behavior.

"Computer Smart," But "People Dumb"

It's amazing that scientists are developing a computer with artificial intelligence which can think for itself. Yet many inventors of these advancements, the computer geniuses, can't get along with their wives and children or the people with whom they work. The more we deal with emotionless machines which do exactly what we program them to do, the less effective we become in relating to living, thinking, feeling people. As our technology becomes more advanced, we need to learn and practice people skills because we can't allow technology to become a substitute for genuine relationships.

We tend to judge others by our values and personalities. Task-oriented individuals often think people-oriented individuals are compromisers. People-oriented folks see task people as insensitive. These differing views simply reveal our unique feelings and attitudes about life. What really matters is how we allow those drives and passions to control us. The "nitty gritty of life" is when we learn to control them. Better yet, God gets the glory when we allow the Holy Spirit to control us.

You've probably heard someone say, "What we need around here is to get organized. The Bible says to do all things decently and in order, and God is not the author of confusion. We shouldn't be sloppy in God's business, His church!" A crowd echoes, "Amen!" They believe the church should be more high tech. They want to get the job done in a bigger, better and more efficient way.

But perhaps you've heard, "I'm sick and tired of programs, projects, and procedures. We just need to love each other." That crowd could not care less about starting or ending meetings on time, agendas, and job descriptions. They're high touch and feel deeply for people. They think it is more spiritual to care and share with others. Actually, the Bible teaches both attitudes. Both have inherent strengths and weaknesses, and both can be used for good or to manipulate or hide. God can use those who are task-oriented and those who are people-oriented, but both can get out of balance.

Some of us feel that others are too wishy washy about convictions. "They talk a lot, care a lot, and feel a lot, but never really accomplish anything great for God." Those who are more sensitive, however, think that the "movers and shakers" are too intolerant, too insensitive, and too pushy. They may get the job done, but they leave a long line of casualties behind.

Both groups need to learn from the other. The high tech crowd needs to be more high touch, and the love group needs to help carry the load in doing the tasks around the church. The church is both an organization and an organism. It needs to work and it needs to worship. It needs to move forward and to minister. Believers should challenge and love one another.

One of the problems which accentuate these differences is our set of assumptions. Each type of person (and indeed, each person) has a set of assumptions which shapes and colors responses to people and situations. One of the factors which shapes our responses to people and circumstances is our pattern of thoughts. In his excellent book, *The Crazy-Making Workplace*, Archibald Hart[1] writes:

> In addition to examining your personality, you need to take a look at the way you think ... Many unhappy people ... can trace their unhappiness to the way they think. They misconstrue

motives of others. They misperceive the actions of others. They misinterpret what people say, twisting it to suit their assumptions. Crooked thinking is what some have called it. Author Zig Ziglar calls it 'stinkin' thinkin',' and he is right on target. A difficult situation or crisis can bring out the worst in our thinking styles. We may assume the reason we feel resentment, guilt, sadness, anger, or jealousy is because of the crisis. We then fail to notice that between the crisis and our emotional reaction, a lot of unhealthy thoughts have intruded to disturb our peace of mind. The crisis in itself has not upset us, but the way we think when we are in crisis has caused our reaction. We react in a split second. What comes out as anger or depression is as much, if not more so, the consequence of our thinking patterns as it is the crisis. If we can catch our thinking and intervene with healthier thoughts, not only will we feel better but we will be more able to take positive, constructive steps to deal with the crisis.[1]

ENDNOTES
[1]Hart, Archibald, *The Crazy-Making Workplace*, (Ann Arbor: Vine Books, 1993), p. 90, 92.

5

The Mystery Of Motivation

There's a mistake and misunderstanding about motivation. People err in thinking motivation is an art. You perhaps have heard about the so-called "art of motivation", but motivation is actually a science. Art is free expression which changes from medium to medium or person to person. Science, on the other hand, is observable and repeatable. Science doesn't change other than in predictable and controlled situations. The "art of motivation" is actually the "science of motivation" because most people have predictable patterns of behavior. Their behavior is obvious and calculable.

Art is also a rendering of reality, not reality itself. A person can paint another person's feelings on canvas, portray them in drama, or express them in many other art forms. The form and expression change according to the medium, the crowd, and the performance, therefore it is more art than science. In science, you can predict the outcome and observe continuity.

The mystery is how to motivate others. Actually, you can't

motivate anyone because everyone is already motivated in his or her own way.

Good motivators are those who do not intimidate or manipulate. Instead, they create the climate and environment that encourages people to do right. That's what a good coach, teacher, parent, boss, preacher, or leader does to get people to respond.

Intimidation & Manipulation

I don't want to be an intimidator or manipulator. I want to be an imitator. I want to be like Christ. I want to exhibit his life in me. "I'm crucified with Christ; nevertheless I live, yet not I, but Christ lives in me and the life I now live in the flesh, I live by the faith of the Son of God, who loved me and gave Himself for me" (Gal. 2:20).

The greatest motivation anyone could have is the love of Christ. In 2 Cor. 5:14, Paul teaches, "For Christ's love compels us" (NIV). The King James Version of the Bible uses a slightly different word: "For the love of Christ constrains us." Both translations indicate the compelling and constraining motivation of the love of Christ. We ought to do what we do, not because of our personalities or spiritual gifts, but because we love Christ and want to obey Him.

Zech. 4:6 reminds us, "It's not by might, nor by power, but by My Spirit,' says the Lord." It's also not by our giftedness, ability, or talents, either. God often uses the foolish things of the world to confound the wise, and the weak things to confound the mighty (1 Cor. 1:27). This is a paradox: How do the foolish things become wise and the weak things become mighty? The principle in Scripture is this: to live, you must first die. In John 12:24, Jesus explains, "Unless a grain of wheat first falls to the ground and dies, it abides alone, but if it dies, it brings forth much fruit." The caterpillar has to first enter and "die" in its casket-type chrysalis in order to resurrect and turn into a beautiful butterfly.

In his book, *13 Fatal Errors Managers Make*, Steven Brown (not the preacher Brown) identifies Error #5 as, "Managing everyone the same way." I am inclined to add: A fatal error parents, preachers, teachers, coaches, salespeople, and counselors make could easily be parenting, preaching, teaching, coaching, selling, and counseling everyone the same way.

"Train Up A Child"

Proverbs 22:6 teaches us, "Train a child in the way he should go, so when he is old he won't depart from it." But there's more to this verse than meets the eye. I believe many of us have mistranslated Prov. 22:6 over the years. The traditional translation is, "Train a child right and he will live right later." How many people do you know who were trained right as children but don't live right later as adults? The problem with the traditional translation is with the words "train," "way," and "it." The key is in the word "it" — "and he won't depart from it." We have traditionally referred the word "it" back to the word "training." Train a child right and he won't depart from it, the training. In the Hebrew text, however, the word "it" can relate back to the word "way." In other words, train a child according to his way or bent and when he is old, he won't depart from it, his way or bent. The word "way" in the Hebrew denotes "bent" or personality. We should raise and train children according to their bents. We should discover every child's personality as soon as possible, and lead him or her accordingly. The lesson is clear. We need to train children according to their personalities because these bents have so much influencing and lasting power in their lives.

Researchers tell us 85% of a child's personality is formed by age 6. By the time children reach the age of 21, their personalities are set. Only what we call S.E.E.s, Significant Emotional Experiences or Significant Emotional Events, change an individual's personality. If you were a happy, go-lucky 21 year-old, you'll probably be a happy- go-lucky 81 year-old. If you were a crabby and complaining

21 year old .... you probably won't live to be 81! There is much to be said about the power of a child's personality, and the need to influence it when the child is very young.

The challenge is to identify children's bents and lead them according to their personalities. The key is knowing how to read people and manage them according to their motivations, not ours. This is what the Apostle Paul meant when he taught, "I've become all things to all men that I might by all means save some" (1 Cor. 9:22). We must learn how to adapt our responses and behavior to the motivations and "bents" of others in order to improve our effectiveness. This is not as easy as it sounds.

Paul's Plight

Learning why people do what they do is an age-old challenge. The Apostle Paul writes in Rom. 7:15, "I don't understand what I do. For what I want to do I do not, but what I hate I do." (That sounds a lot like me!) Have you ever told yourself to be careful you don't say a certain thing in the heat of an argument, and then you end up saying it? Or have you ever just hung up the phone, or walked away from a difficult situation in which strong feelings were shared and you wished you had said something else, or you rehearse in your mind what you should have said?

I believe Paul is wrestling with his feelings and responses to the trying times of life. He introduces us to the deadly dilemma everyone faces: How do we respond to our natural feelings in light of God's laws? Paul begins by painting a picture of the conflict within everyone. James also explains how the trials and troubles, the interpersonal conflicts of life, start from within. "Why do we fight and quarrel? Don't they come from our lusts (desires) that war within our members (selves)" (James 4:1). Most of our people-problems begin with some kind of conflict over the way we feel, think, or act, as opposed to the way someone else feels, thinks, or acts. The way we are wired doesn't connect with the way others are wired.

Paul continues by introducing us to the "I" and "me" in him. Paul writes, "For when I want to do good, sin is present with me." Who are the "I" and "me" Paul refers to? He also explains, "It's not I, but sin that dwells in me." I believe Paul is explaining the conflict between his personality, Paul's "I," and the old adamic sin nature, his "me." Our personalities are neither good, nor bad. They are neutral. It's what we do with our personalities that is good or bad. You may be thinking, "Mels, you haven't met my next door neighbor, or boss, or mother-in-law. They have 'bad personalities'!" But no one has a bad personality.

Paul adds, "For I know what is within me (that is in my flesh)" (vs. 18). Notice Paul makes it clear he is not referring to the "I" in him, his personality. He's focusing on the "me" in him, his flesh, the old adamic nature that causes his problems. Remember, you don't have to teach a baby to be selfish. It comes naturally. At the same time, you don't have to teach people to feel bad when they do wrong. God has put within all of us a policeman, judge, and school master— a conscience— to teach us we're sinners in need of a Savior.

There are laws at work in each of us. The law of sin and death is working on our personality through our sinful nature to make us do wrong. The commandments which are written on our hearts are our God-consciousness which points us to Christ. "We would have never known sin, had it not been for the law" (Rom. 7:7). The law can't save us, but it sure does make us feel guilty when we sin so we will look to Christ for forgiveness.

The dilemma develops as we see Paul struggling with these two laws at work within him. In this terrible struggle, Paul cries, "O wretched man that I am, who shall deliver me from the body of this death" (Rom. 7:24).

"Who," Not "Why," Is More Important

I'm so glad Paul asked, "who" will deliver us — not "what," "why," "when," or "how." We often ask the wrong questions. It's okay to ask, "what, why, when, or how," but God is not obligated to answer these questions. I don't want to alarm you, but God didn't even answer His own son, Jesus, when He cried from the cross, "My God, My God, why have you forsaken me?" The only question God is obligated to answer is the "who" question. I don't know "what" the future holds, but I know "who" holds the future. I don't know "why" bad things happen to good people, but I know "who" knows why.

Perhaps this is why they call the owl, "the wise old owl," because he asks the right questions: "Who? Who? Who?" Paul wrote to Timothy, "For I know whom I have believed and am persuaded that He is able to keep that which I have committed unto Him, against that day" (2 Timothy 1:12).

When Paul cried, "Who shall deliver me from the body of this death," he agonized over the emotions of this struggle. The term, "the body of this death," refers to an unusual kind of capital punishment in that day. The typical punishment was crucifixion or stoning to death, but occasionally, people convicted of the capital murder crime were punished by having the victim's corpse tied to their back — wrist to wrist, waist to waist, and ankle to ankle, until the dead, decaying corpse eventually spread disease and killed the convicted murderer. Paul graphically expresses the deadly dilemma of his personality in the middle between the struggling forces of the law of sin and the law of God.

The solution to this problem, "who shall deliver me?" is simple, yet profound. This is like the bad news that makes the Good News good. The Good News is in the next verse. In Rom. 7:25, Paul answers his question, "Thanks be to God, through Jesus Christ our Lord." Christ is the answer to our conflicts. It sounds so simple, but it is truly profound. Trusting Christ is the simplest thing anyone could ever do. He did all the work. There's nothing we can do to add or take away from what He has already done. Remember, He said, "It is finished" (John 19:30).

The Good News

The gospel is clear: "For by grace are you saved through faith, and that not of yourselves. It is the gift of God, not of works, so that no one can boast" (Eph. 2:8,9). All anyone can do is to rely on Christ as the one who died and rose again to pay the complete penalty for sin, then you can know for certain you have eternal life (1 John 5:13). You will never have to wonder or worry again where you will spend eternity, because your security is in Christ.

The Bible speaks of two kinds of belief. Most people believe Christ existed. Even "the devil believes and trembles" (James 2:19), but the biblical word for "belief" is more than a mental assent to a historical fact. Christ died, that's history. But Christ died for me, that's salvation. Believing in Christ as your Savior means putting your complete faith and trust in His finished work on the cross. He also rose again to validate your faith. It's not faith in a dead savior or religious leader. It's faith in a living Lord who rose again for your justification (proof of redemption) (Rom. 4:25).

When you trust Christ as your Savior, you enter into a new relationship with God. He comes into your life by invitation, by faith alone. He is not a bully. He is not rude. He will never force His way into anyone's life. You must trust Him to come in, but He who created the universe is not interested in just being an invited guest. He wants to be the host, to make decisions like how to rearrange the furniture of your life, decisions that guarantee not only eternal life but abundant life. And He who created the universe is not just interested in being the host in your life, He wants to be head! He wants to be the Lord of your life, your feelings, thoughts, and actions.

Christ comes into our lives, forgives our sins, and then demands we obey Him as Lord, not in order to be saved, but out of thankfulness because we are saved. Heaven actually begins the moment you trust Christ. You don't have to die to experience heaven. It starts the moment you receive the free gift of eternal life and then allow Him to be the Lord of your life. Trusting Christ will take you to heaven, but obeying Him will bring heaven to you. The question is: What are you going to do with Christ? Are you going to let Him be the Lord of your giftedness, feelings, thoughts, and actions?

Notice in Rom. 8:1, "There is, therefore, now no condemnation to those who are in Christ Jesus." Trusting Christ is the solution to the deadly dilemma between the flesh and the commandments, the law of sin and the law of God. These two laws cause war and conflict in our lives. Paul then introduces us to another law, the law of the Spirit. Remember, the law of the flesh destroys and the law of God is too weak to save us, but the law of the Spirit liberates us from the law of sin and death (Rom. 8:3).

When I go to church, I'm not attending a funeral or some dead meeting. I've come to celebrate the risen Savior! He's alive and living in me. I don't attend church, give, and serve because I have to, but because I want to. It's the most exciting thing in the world to live by the law of the Spirit. I don't do what I do because of rules, regulations, or rituals, but because of the reality of Christ in my life. I don't obey the Scriptures because of tradition, but because of the truth within me, the joy of sins forgiven, and the assurance of eternal life. "And you shall know the truth and the truth shall set you free" (John 8:32).

Keep Looking Down

I love to tell people, "Keep looking down!" Everybody always responds, "What do you mean, 'looking down'? I need to keep looking up." And I share, "You don't have to look up when you're already up. You're seated with Christ in the heavenlies "above all principalities and powers" (Eph. 2:6, Eph. 1:20 and 21). Remember your position in Christ. You're "more than conquerors" (Rom. 8:37). I've read the last chapter. I've fast forwarded the tape to the end. We win! We end up on top. We're victorious in Christ. Keep looking down!

In the next section, we're going to look at the practical side of why so many people who are victorious in Christ can fail so terribly in relationships. Why do those who experience God in church then act like the devil at work or home when it comes to solving their people-problems. How can we be so theologically smart, yet people dumb?

Part 2

Understanding Natural Gifts

6

An Ancient Discovery For Modern Times

The terms personality and temperament are synonymous. When we use these terms, we're referring to patterns of thoughts, feelings, and behaviors. There are many theories about personality types. After much study, I chose to use the DISC Model because it's simple to understand, easy to remember, and practical to apply.

Understanding our active or passive roles helps us identify our specific temperament styles. By combining these two different categories of influences (active/passive and task/people), we end up with four specific types.

Everyone has a predictable pattern of behavior because of his or her specific personality. There are four basic personality types. These types, also known as temperaments, blend together to determine your unique personality. To help you understand why you often feel, think and act the way you do, the following graphic summarizes the Four Temperament Model of Human Behavior.

Graphically, we see the following four temperament types:

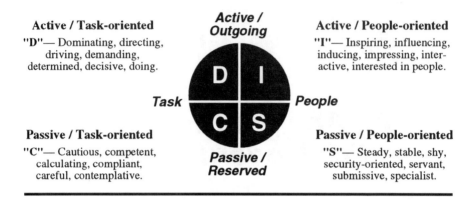

Active / Task-oriented

"**D**"— Dominating, directing, driving, demanding, determined, decisive, doing.

Active / Outgoing

Active / People-oriented

"**I**"— Inspiring, influencing, inducing, impressing, interactive, interested in people.

Task

People

Passive / Task-oriented

"**C**"— Cautious, competent, calculating, compliant, careful, contemplative.

Passive / Reserved

Passive / People-oriented

"**S**"— Steady, stable, shy, security-oriented, servant, submissive, specialist.

Some people are easily identifiable as active extroverts or passive introverts, but many of us are confused because not all extroverts are active toward people. Some are active in tasks. In the same way, introverts can be passive in relation to people or tasks. Understanding the four quadrant model of basic human behavior sheds light on this. It can make the difference between the right and wrong response and a proper or improper behavior in any given situation.

Hippocrates, the father of modern medicine, first observed four unique temperament types, or four specific patterns of behavior. (See page 257 for more background). He thought it had something to do with the chemical makeup of the blood. To describe the four types, he used Greek words which have been Anglicized as: choleric, sanguine, phlegmatic, and melancholy. Many others who observe human behavior have categorized people into four temperaments, but personality types have nothing to do with the color of body fluids! Temperaments are a mixture of nature and nurture. You can correlate the Greek terms to the DISC model:

- "D" is the Choleric.
- "I" is the Sanguine.
- "S" is the Phlegmatic.
- "C" is the Melancholy.

A Quick Look

Our personalities should never become an excuse for poor behavior. The attitude of many is, "That's just the way I am. Love me or leave me. You knew I was like that when you married me," but we shouldn't blame our rotten reactions on our personalities.

Each temperament style represents a specific behavior pattern. How we use or abuse our personalities determines our effectiveness with others. Once we understand the four quadrant model of behavior styles, we can begin to identify our individual profile. To simplify the four types of temperaments, we will use William Marston's DISC titles. The following are the four quadrants of the DISC model:

- "D" — active / task-oriented
- "I" — active / people-oriented
- "S" — passive / people-oriented
- "C" — passive / task-oriented

DISC Descriptions

Here's a simple description of each of the four types of behavior represented by the letters D-I-S-C. A strong or high type behavior is more obvious and predictable than a weak or low type.

"D" Behavior—

"D"s are determined leaders. They can take control of a situation, make quick decisions, and cause things to happen. If they overuse their strengths, they can become dictatorial, demanding, or domineering.

The apostle Paul was a "D" type. He was unmovable, relentless, and dedicated, perhaps more than any other man in the New Testament.

"I" Behavior—

High "I"s are optimistic people who lead by inspiring, influencing, and inducing others to follow. They may be characterized by overconfidence, talkativeness, and a craving for popularity. These individuals tend to compromise their beliefs due to peer pressure.

Peter is a good example of an "I." He is often found speaking for the group: excited and outspoken.

"S" Behavior—

High "S"s are stable, submissive, and steady. They don't like change and are extremely loyal. The most tolerant of all, these people are often timid and too agreeable.

Moses demonstrated "S" behavior. He was pessimistic about his ability to lead the people out of Egypt, but he was faithful and steady as their leader.

"C" Behavior—

Strong "C"s are cautious, calculating, and conservative. They are seldom wrong because they are slow to decide. However, these individuals tend to overanalyze and be too critical of others.

Thomas is perhaps the best biblical illustration of a "C." He doubted and questioned, but when Jesus showed him His hands and side, Thomas became thoroughly convinced.

Strengths and Weaknesses

Each personality has its strengths and weaknesses. Conflict or harmony in relationships are the result of how we use or abuse our personalities in response to life's situations. Proverbs 30:11-14 describes four types of generations. Each is presented negatively, and each is different from the other:

- The generation of children that curse their fathers and do not bless their mothers (v. 11) is like the "C." Their weakness is a critical spirit.
- Pure in their own eyes, the next generation (v. 12) is like the "S" who seldom does wrong or offends anyone. Some people, however, need to be told the truth even at the risk of offending them. Scripture admonishes us to be careful when all men speak well of us and when we try to please everyone.
- The generation with lofty eyes lifted up (v. 13) is like the "I" type. They prefer to be seen and to show off.
- The "D" generation is like those whose teeth are as swords (v. 14). They are fighters and have little sympathy for others.

These warnings imply that each of us has the potential of being a blessing or a curse to others. We can be pure in God's eyes or man's eyes. We can lift ourselves up or let God lift us up. We can flee conflict, we can be fighters, or we can be faithful to do as God would have us do.

Keep in mind that 85% of people tend to be composites of DISC, therefore, most people will be blends and combinations of the characteristics evident in the four personalities. There are numerous variations of this model. Speakers, writers, and trainers have added their own titles to make the model more simple or personal, but this four vector explanation of basic human behavior has become universally recognized. The DISC personality profile was originally designed by Dr. John Geier and has been validated by the Kaplan Report and Winchester Report. The DISC profile and Model of Human Behavior stand out as the most reliable and practical available today.

Basic Overview of the DISC Model

Psychologist Dr. Frank Wichern introduced me to a full description of the four temperament types while I attended Dallas Theological Seminary. I want to include his insights here, which I have modified in a few places.[1] You may want to add characteristics to this list as you learn more about people's patterns of behavior.

High "D"s

BASIC MOTIVATION:
- Challenge

ENVIRONMENT NEEDS:
- Freedom
- Authority
- Varied activities
- Difficult assignments
- Opportunity for advancement

RESPONDS BEST TO A LEADER WHO:
- Provides direct answers
- Sticks to business
- Stresses goals
- Provides pressure
- Allows freedom for personal accomplishment

NEEDS TO LEARN THAT:
- People are important
- Relaxation is not a crime
- Some controls are needed
- Everyone has a boss
- Verbalizing conclusions helps other people understand them better

High "I"s

BASIC MOTIVATION:
- Recognition

ENVIRONMENT NEEDS:
- Prestige
- Friendly relationships
- Opportunities to influence others
- Opportunities to inspire people
- Chance to verbalize ideas

RESPONDS BEST TO A LEADER WHO:
- Is a democratic manager and a friend
- Provides social involvement outside of work
- Provides recognition of abilities
- Offers incentives for risk-taking

NEEDS TO LEARN THAT:
- Time must be managed
- There is such a thing as too much optimism
- Details are important
- Humility is a virtue

High "S"s

BASIC MOTIVATION:
- Security

ENVIRONMENT NEEDS:
- An area of specialization
- Identification with a group
- Established work pattern
- Stability of situation
- Consistent, familiar environment

RESPONDS BEST TO A LEADER WHO:
- Is relaxed and amiable
- Allows time to adjust to change in plans
- Serves as a friend
- Allows people to work at their own pace
- Answers "how" questions
- Clearly defines goals and means of reaching them
- Gives personal support

NEEDS TO LEARN THAT:
- Change provides opportunity
- Friendship isn't everything
- Discipline is good

High "C"s

BASIC MOTIVATION:
• Quality

ENVIRONMENT NEEDS:
• Clearly defined tasks
• Sufficient time and resources to accomplish tasks
• Explanations
• Team participation
• Limited risks
• Assignments that require precision and planning

RESPONDS BEST TO A LEADER WHO:
• Provides reassurance
• Maintains a supportive atmosphere
• Provides open door policy
• Defines concise, detailed operating standards

NEEDS TO LEARN THAT:
• Total support is not always necessary
• Thorough explanation is not always possible
• Deadlines must be met

People respond to discovering their personality types in many different ways. Some people find it fascinating; others find it frustrating. For some, identifying their temperaments is easy. For others, it can be extremely difficult. Some people are more obviously one or two personality types, but others are a complex blend. If your personality fits into one or two categories, it is easier to identify and understand your specific personality. Most people quickly recognize their strengths and uniquenesses, but some feel they are a little of every type. This may cause confusion. Evaluation is not always easy, so be honest with yourself and focus on those characteristics which are obvious. Disregard the descriptions which don't fit. Narrow it down to one or two types which best describe you.

Your personality even shapes your response to this study. "D"s are sometimes proud of their type. "I"s tend to be more excited and talkative about their personality. "S"s are more shy and quiet. "C"s are usually the most doubtful and confused.

I often have people come to me after a seminar and say, "Is this really valid? I don't know if I agree with my profile."

I respond, "I can prove how valid it is. You're a High "C", aren't you?"

They invariably look surprised and ask, "How did you know?"

And I explain, "C's always ask the same questions. They doubt the validity and need more explanation."

Some people are afraid to identify their personalities. I try to reassure them that their assessment is not a test and there are no wrong answers. They can't fail it. It simply profiles their personality types, and no one has a bad personality. A few people have had bad experiences with psychological testing, and they feel hesitant to try another tool. Basic temperament assessment, however, is not a clinical measurement. It is designed for people who simply want to understand a little more about themselves and others. People who struggle most over personality profiling are often pessimistic about themselves. They sometimes suffer from poor self-images. They have trouble seeing their personalities as God's unique gift to them, and they are afraid of change and control.

To get the most out of self-discovery and self-acceptance, we need to recognize how God is working to mold and make us like Christ. When we don't understand our strengths and weaknesses, we have difficulty knowing how He will guide us and use us. God's shaping process inevitably affects our motivations, behavior, and relationships. Realize that God used different types of people throughout Scripture to do His work. Relate to each biblical and contemporary example as it applies to your life. Above all, trust God to help you become the person He wants you to be.

In his bestselling book, *The Search for Significance*, Robert McGee describes the purpose and the process of depending on the Holy Spirit to fill us and change us. He writes:

> Paul wrote to the Galatian Christians: " . . . the fruit of the Spirit is love, joy, peace, patience, kindness, goodness, faithfulness, gentleness, and self-control . . ." As we respond to the love of Christ and trust His Spirit to fill us, these characteristics will become increasingly evident in our lives. The filling of the Holy Spirit includes two major aspects: our purpose (to bring honor to Christ instead of ourselves) and our resources (trusting His love and power to accomplish results instead of trusting in our own wisdom and abilities). Although we will continue to mature in our relationship with the Lord over the years, we can begin to experience His love, strength, and purpose from the moment we put Him at the center of our lives.[2]

I have known Christian leaders who sincerely believe Jesus is the Lord of their lives, who are biblical scholars, who sacrificially give and serve in their churches, and who would claim to be mature in Christ, but who also fight like cats and dogs with everybody! They teach about how rich we are in Christ, but they are paupers when it comes to having people skills. All Christians, especially our spiritual leaders, should learn how to read others and enjoy working more effectively with people.

Rocky, Sparky, Susie, and Claire

To illustrate the importance of understanding others, picture a teacher asking his or her class the simple question, "Who discovered America?" There are all different types of personalities in the class.

Rocky, the high "D" yells out, "Columbus. Next question!"

The teacher responds, "Why did you yell out like that, Rocky? Why don't you raise your hand like everyone else?"

Rocky likes to take charge. He wants to be in control. He wants to get everything done in a hurry so he can go play.

The teacher asks again, "Who discovered America?" Sparky, the high "I" jumps up, waving his hand, and says, "I know, I know. Call on me, teacher! Please!"

She responds, "Okay, Sparky, who discovered America?"

He acts like he knows, but says, "Oh, I forgot. It's right on the tip of my tongue. Can you give me the first letter?"

He wants to turn it into a game like Wheel Of Fortune. He asks, "Can I buy a vowel?"

The teacher sighs, "Oh Sparky, put your hand down and stop acting like a clown. Why do you always raise your hand without having anything say?"

Sparky responds with a surprised silly face and sits down while the class laughs at his antics.

The teacher then asks Susie, the high "S", "Who do you think discovered America?"

Softly Susie says, "I think it's Columbus, but I'm not sure. If anyone else knows and wants to say, it's okay with me. And if you don't like Columbus, I'm sorry. I hope this doesn't make anyone mad."

Finally, the teacher asks Claire, the high "C", "Do you know who discovered America?"

Claire gives the teacher one of those disgusting glares and blurts out, "Now what do you mean by that question?"

Rocky explodes, "Come on, Claire! Why do you make a

mountain out of a mole hill. Let's finish this nonsense so we can go play!"

Rocky loves recess. He considers himself King of the Playground. He tells everybody, "We're going to play kickball today. I'm captain." And pointing to friend, says, "And you're captain of the other team."

Another strong-willed student interrupts, "I don't want to play kickball. And who made you captain anyway?"

That's a "D" challenging another "D." (That's how you start new churches!)

Sparky gets all excited. He says, "I love it when Rocky is about to get into a fight." Sparky yells, "Ding, round two," like the ring announcer at a boxing match.

Poor Susie covers her face and begins to cry. Sobbing she says, "I'm sorry. I'm sorry. I didn't know it was going to upset everyone. Please forgive me and don't fight."

Finally Claire screams, "Now wait a minute! What about the native American Indians? They were here before Columbus. What about the Vikings? They were also here before Columbus. You need to be more clear with your question!"

Every child responded according to his or her personality. Each one had a predictable pattern of behavior. This is an age-old truth with very modern applications.

In the following chapters, we'll examine each of the four personality types in more detail.

ENDNOTES
[1]Used by permission.
[2]McGee, Robert S., *The Search for Significance*, (Houston: Rapha, 1990), p. 134.

7

Controlling The Dominant Personality

When you think of the people who seem to be natural leaders, who accept challenges, who are involved in many different projects, and who are more task- than people-oriented, you are thinking of high "D"s.

"D"s are:
- Dominant,
- Direct,
- Determined,
- Demanding,
- Doers.

"D"s push for results. They shape the environment by overcoming opposition. They are very active, and they create aggressive environments, striving and pushing under pressure to get the job done. Also known as the "Rocky Cholerics," they're the rough, tough Rambo types. They love action-oriented challenges. "D"s tend to cause action or trouble, depending on how they respond to stress. They constantly question the status quo. Their motto is, "If it doesn't work, change it." They take charge; they want to be in control. They were most likely the self-appointed captains of teams (or even leaders of gangs) growing up.

"D"s are often raised to dominate and direct the action of others. Apart from God, fathers and mothers are the greatest influences in shaping behavior. Parents who possess strong leadership qualities and determined personalities tend to produce high "D" children.

"D"s want control and authority. They often believe they know how to do things better than anyone else and instinctively take charge, but they also work well under authority if they respect their superiors and remember who's the boss.

These determined people need challenge and prestige to fulfill their dreams. They seek opportunities for individual accomplishments and work their way to the top. They become CEOs, owners of their own businesses, or top managers in any field, club, or organization. Even if they don't climb the corporate ladder, "D"s end up telling everyone what to do. They can be found ordering others how to dig a ditch or organizing a local union.

The Apostle Paul's Personality

Before Paul became the great apostle, he was Saul of Tarsus, a persecutor of the church. He was bold, assertive, aggressive, demanding, and driving. After his salvation experience, he was still bold, assertive, aggressive, demanding, and driving, but now he blessed the church rather than curse it. His personality didn't change. It came under God's control.

We see Paul's strong "D" type personality in his "pressing toward the mark, the high calling of God" in Philippians 3:13. He didn't let anything distract him. Paul was almost stoned to death, imprisoned, hated, and forsaken, but he didn't waver. He confronted Peter. He refused to compromise concerning John Mark's involvement in a missionary journey. Paul even made reference to his "weighty letters" (2 Corinthians 10:10) which called people to a radical commitment to Christ.

The apostle was naturally strong, but learned to be sensitive and caring through the filling power of the Holy Spirit. An illustration of his ability to respond to adversity is seen when he was a captive aboard a ship to Lasea, (Acts 27:8-44). A storm arose, and everyone on board feared for their lives. Anticipating a shipwreck, Paul's captors cried out for help. Paul was supposed to be a powerless prisoner, but everyone knew he was a strong leader. He went from being a captive to captain of the ship. Paul went from chains to being in charge.

The most important lesson Paul ever learned was to be controlled by the Spirit. He learned brokenness on the road to Damascus. He learned yieldedness in three years of instruction before beginning his ministry and again in his thirteen year sabbatical. God crushed and conquered Paul to make him a great crusader for Christ. Paul's greatest need was learning how to control himself before he tried to influence others. The Lord used strong measures to teach these lessons. Out of control, Paul was like Saul of Tarsus—reckless and wretched, but under the control of the Spirit, Paul was perhaps the most powerful and effective minister in the history of the church.

Dictators Or Doormats?

"D"s are definitely not doormats. They don't like anyone to step on them. They tend to be dictatorial, and they would be more effective if they would develop skills of delegation. They have the ability to dream, but they usually aren't strong in following through with the details. Therefore, these visionaries need to be able to delegate what they feel is mundane or time consuming.

Paul taught young Timothy, "The things you have heard and learned of me, the same commit thou to faithful men, who shall be able to teach others also" (2 Timothy 2:2). Appearing omnipotent, "D"s push toward their goals without concern for the feelings of others. This is the their greatest strength and greatest weakness. In adversity, they rise to the occasion, but they often unknowingly hurt people in the process.

Though everyone forsook the apostle Paul, the Lord stood with him and strengthened him (2 Timothy 4:16). My question here is, "Why did everyone forsake him?" If it was for his dedication to the Lord, then fine. But I wonder if Paul turned some people off because of his unbending attitude. He didn't have to be abrasive to accomplish his purposes. Not even Jesus had everyone forsake Him. Mary and John stayed with Him even at the cross.

Paul wasn't perfect. He may have been wrong about John Mark. He may have been a little too strong with Peter. I am in no position to specifically criticize Paul, but he was a fallible human being. In spite of his overbearing personality, he is still my hero. I identify with him perhaps more than anyone in the New Testament, but I don't want to pick up his faults as I learn from his strengths.

For "D"s, stumbling blocks are stepping stones. Nothing is too difficult. They want freedom from controls and supervision, so they often become their own bosses. They move fast and hard and are the most prone to become workaholics. Confronted with conflicts, they are quick problem-solvers, but they seldom calculate all the risks or consider all the options.

"D"s are instinctively impatient. They don't put off until tomorrow what they can do today. They push forward despite time limitations. Often misunderstood because of their active, task-oriented, optimistic personalities, these driven individuals are often tough skinned and hard nosed. They act as if the world is going to end tomorrow, therefore the project or plan must be finished today! Their emotions can be extremely intense.

Solomon's High "D" Behavior

King Solomon in the Old Testament was able to do what his father David could not do: build the temple. Solomon was a developer. He was the richest man on earth (2 Chronicles 9:22). He had the ability to make things happen. Forty-one times in the first two chapters of Ecclesiastes, Solomon refers to himself in the first person. He recognized the futility of accomplishments without God's approval. Solomon was a doer, but he learned that "doing without devotion is dearth." Life is empty and shallow if all you do is accomplish things. There is more to life than success.

Having a vision without seeing through spiritual eyes is vanity. Solomon's drive to build the temple was often shortsighted. He manipulated people to accomplish the task. He entered into a covenant with Hiram, but he didn't keep his promise. He negotiated for territories by compromising contracts. His determination to get the job done often got in the way of his dedication to God.

"D"s sometimes seem to accomplish the impossible. They aren't quitters; these driven people love a challenge and are very competitive. They have a "do or die" attitude toward life. As active extroverts, they like to be where the action is; they are unable to stand still for long periods of time. Most of all, they love to direct the action of others. As task-oriented individuals, "D"s absorb themselves in projects rather than people. Often they seem to intimidate people to accomplish their jobs. They use people to build their work rather than use their work to build people. It's not that they don't care about people. They're just more concerned about the projects. People are a means to the end of getting the job done. "D"s appear cold and hard, but God's pruning process can cause them to be more tolerant and caring. Experience and maturity teach them to be more people-oriented.

Dominant types are impatient and easily irritated by those who are indecisive. They like strong leadership. They are purpose-driven. They love challenges, so conflict is normal for them. They seem to relish debate and defiance. Tell "D"s they can't do something, and a startling metamorphosis begins to take place. They can turn into monsters! They attack!

They need to be more calm and understanding of other's feelings. "D"s are often too straightforward and frank. They need to think before reacting. To improve their effectiveness in relationships, these people must control themselves rather than trying to control others.

Domineering Partners

Two "D"s married to each other struggle for control. Ultimately, one will dominate, while the other reluctantly submits to survive. In working relationships, two dominant people jockey for position until someone wins the coveted place of being on top.

I heard about a high "D" pastor of a church with two "D"s on the board of elders. It was obvious from the start that these three men would clash sooner or later! When the pastor came, the church had no budget. The elders wanted a strong leader, but when the pastor introduced the need for a budget at one of the first meetings, the high "D" treasurer took offense. He saw himself as a leader in the church, and anything the pastor said about how money was spent was a personal affront to him. After a few years of this simmering feud, the treasurer became less involved.

At one point, an elder insisted all board members attend Sunday and Wednesday evening services as examples to the rest of the congregation. The pastor agreed and challenged everyone at the next elder's meeting. As expected, the other high "D" had a fit. He resigned. (The pastor didn't think he would get that upset!) The pastor knew the chairman of the elder board, the recognized leader of leaders, agreed with him, and he counted on this man to come to his defense if anything went wrong. But did he? No chance! Not at all! The pastor was unaware that the board members had been individually discussing his leadership style. They concluded he was too strong, too demanding, too "D."

These were all good men. They all loved the Lord and believed the Bible from cover to cover. The pastor's mistake was believing they would communicate with him according to Matthew 18 and 1 Timothy 5 concerning any problem they had. But they didn't, and you can imagine the conflicts these men eventually had! The pastor worked hard to reach the lost, disciple the believers, and feed the flock, but his personality must have chaffed the board. The church was growing rapidly, but the pastor's relationship with the board was going downhill fast!

Unfortunately, the pastor didn't realize how bad it was until a friend told him one of the elders was spending a lot of time with another pastor. The rumor mills buzzed with the idea that this other pastor would replace him. The pastor was anxious and angry. He confronted the elder, but he denied ever talking to the pastor about replacing him. The pastor's high "D" personality had come face to face with that elder's high "D." Somebody had to go!

When you're the new man on the block and truly want peace at all cost, you know who has to bow. For the sake of his family, church friends, and the even the board, the pastor resigned. But God was not finished with him. He used that experience to remind the pastor who really is boss. Not the pastor. Not the board. But Him. And if he would sincerely allow Him to be the Lord of all his hurts, misunderstanding, and even wrongs, he could become better, not bitter.

The only difference in the words "bitter" and "better" is the letter "i." Each of us must answer for our actions, thoughts, and feelings. God is conforming us into the image of Christ, so we must concentrate on our shortcomings, not the wrongs of others.

After all is said from both sides of any conflict, only you can decide to do right. You can't force others to accept your humble apology for how you have disappointed them. You can't make them admit their wrongs. As "D"s, we shouldn't try to control each other. In the conflict at the church in this story, the men should have loved and respected each other in spite of each other's faults.

Who's The Boss?

A high "D" will try to control someone with a low "D" score and make all the decisions. The other often sheepishly obeys. Low "D"s willingly follow along in submission until their most serious concerns are challenged.

Sarah tried to control Abraham by insisting that Hagar bear the heir, and she laughed at God when He promised she would be the mother of the child even though she was far past her childbearing years. She resisted her husband, but she was an example of humility after God proved His faithfulness to her.

Low "D" people find it very difficult to confront high "D"s. Their best preparation for battle is accurate information to prove their point. Presenting high "D"s with analysis usually causes them to look more closely at the conflict and be more rational.

As parents, "D"s are usually domineering and demand a lot of their children. They are strong in discipline. They lean toward absolutes; everything is "right or wrong," and compromise is uncomfortable.

In marriage, two dominant people need to learn to communicate clearly and respect each other's goals and desires. I recently met two "D"s who had been married for some time. They were both strong willed and aggressive. Their marriage had become void of feelings. Little communication existed, but they seemed fairly happy. I honestly wondered, "How can they be happy?" They explained they never made a major decision unless they both agreed. It seemed to work, and I was impressed. It's uncommon for the marriage of two "D"s to survive through childraising, buying homes, and growing old because they often feel pressured by the other. The trials and troubles of life often prove too great a strain on the relationship because they both have to win.

In his book, *Trusting*, Pat Springle describes how dominating people have difficulties in their spiritual lives. He writes:

> 'Domineering people' have problems relating to God. After all, only one person can take charge of the universe. And how can someone be submissive when his or her entire life is dedicated to dominating everyone and everything? . . . Tension between the desire to dominate and the desire to look humble creates internal conflicts of major proportions. This inner struggle can be resolved by avoiding the threat of intimacy and focusing on analysis and action. Instead of experiencing the love, grace, and gentleness of God, aggressive people analyze it. They may study every major doctrinal issue so they can understand it thoroughly—and dominate any discussion. While analysis is not as rich and fulfilling as genuine experience, it's certainly not as threatening. These individuals settle for a business relationship with God: 'You do your part, God, and I'll do mine. You can count on me, and I sure hope I can count on you.'[1]

Under pressure, our strengths become our weaknesses. We're more comfortable and confident in roles, qualities, and abilities we know best. A "D" tends to become more dominant and demanding under pressure. When the going gets tough, the "D"s get going . . .

right for the jugular! They tend to steamroll and subdue their opposition, and force of character is often their style of confronting. "Do something! Lead, follow, or get out of the way!" is their approach to dealing with stress. Their leadership ability is an attribute, but carried to an extreme, it becomes dictatorial.

In many situations, someone needs to take charge. All Indians and no chief usually means mass chaos and confusion, and "D"s are glad to be the chiefs. They are decisive leaders, and in emergencies, their powers of thinking and making decisions are heightened. They go from zero to hero or hero to zero, depending on how they handle the challenge.

Nehemiah's determination to build the wall around Jerusalem brought all sorts of adversity, but he pressed on. He was able to rally the people and organize them into units to finish the task in a fraction of the time most people expected. "D"s need others who can rationally weigh pros and cons in stressful situations. Nehemiah had his advisors. Paul learned from Aquilla and Priscilla. As risk-takers, "D"s must learn to stop long enough to calculate the risks. They should become more cautious in their actions and more gentle and caring in relationships. Free-spirited, these visionary people need a structured environment. They're predictably unpredictable, changing rules in the middle of the game because of expedience.

Doers, Not Thinkers

"D"s' greatest influence over others is their ability to accomplish goals. Though careless at times, they usually still produce results. They tend to make people nervous because they are producers, pushers, and movers. They make great achievers if they don't self-destruct. They often speak before thinking, but surprisingly, they often come up with unique and immediate solutions. These results give them the confidence to "fly by the seat of their pants." Other people, however, don't feel comfortable with this free-wheel-ing style, so "D"s need to be more considerate of others. Dominant, demanding people tend to overlook little things that make others feel apprehensive. Absorbed in task-oriented projects, they cause high casualty rates among subordinates and co-workers. Their "herd mentality" of getting everyone moving in the same direction at the same time is demeaning to others who prefer to be treated as individuals.

"D"s are sometimes great motivators and challenging speakers, but their greatest concern is "reaching the mark, not touching the heart." By learning to balance their penchant for tasks with concern for people, "D"s can be much more effective leaders. Paul did this by his back door approach in his sermon on Mars Hill in Athens. He could have told everyone how stupid they were, but instead he convincingly confronted them with a contrast of Christ. He pulled his punches by not condemning their false idols.

Though "D"s occasionally delegate work, they usually feel compelled to do everything themselves to maintain control and have it done "the right way." Once they learn to spread the responsibility around, they should supervise—but not smother—those who are contributing to the task. One of their biggest faults is taking back delegated responsibility. To "save" a project, they may take back control and offend the one who was placed in charge. "D"s need to learn to communicate the purpose, plan, and process more effectively with others. Unfortunately, they believe the myth that everyone else thinks and feels as they do.

"D"s prefer techniques based on practical experience. Though they are pragmatic, they tend to theorize too much. More detailed approaches would improve their results.

Remembering biblical ethics and scriptural principles is imperative. They tend to lose sight of truth while focusing on the finish line. Winning at the expense of character is a defeat with a crown. Success apart from the proper means is a loss. Paul crudely compared it to "dung" (Philippians 3:8).

"D"s are tireless workers in the church, but they can become too task-oriented, too demanding, and too decisive. They need to remember that only a few people are like them. Most people are more sensitive and thoughtful. Typically insensitive, demanding people will markedly increase their effectiveness by being more people-oriented. God often uses "D"s in the church as change agents, but most people don't want change. "D" pastors are often misunderstood. Their dreams and drives scare people, but when they earn respect and trust, they can lead the church to great heights.

An occasional shock brings confident, dominant individuals back to earth. Experience is their best teacher, and their overconfidence is tempered by the painful consequences of bad decisions from time to time. To be most successful, they need difficult assignments. They are easily bored and need constant challenge, but they need to stay focused on the most important task and see it through to the end.

Jesus chose twelve disciples. Gideon reduced his army to only three hundred men. Paul poured his life into individuals. We see each of these leaders' "D" behavior challenging crowds but focusing on individuals. The results were evident as they learned the principle of "being as big as all but as small as one."

Slow Down and Explain

Once a decision is made on how a task should be accomplished, "D"s should tell others the reasons behind their decisions. Though they may be convinced and confident of that decision, others may not be. Clear and patient explanations enhance a person's role in leadership. It's not enough to simply say, "Because!" or "I'm the boss!" Reasons and specific plans need to be verbalized for everyone to feel secure in the decision.

"D"s are often like the Pony Express: Nothing can stop them! They need to pace themselves and learn to relax. Vacations provide the needed balance for their high stress levels. Physical conditioning is vital because stress is one of their worst enemies! They are often unaware of the tremendous pressure they put on themselves to produce, and they are prime candidates for heart attacks and hypertension. Learning to relax and enjoy life should be part of their plans to succeed. Vance Havner said, "If we don't learn to come apart for a while and rest, we may just come apart!"

Most importantly, these driven people need to learn to prioritize. Working overtime and seldom pausing to appreciate their mates and children is hazardous to their health and wealth. The twin tyrannies of urgency and expedience are dilemmas they must avoid.

As weekend mechanics with finely tuned machines, "D"s seem to race through life without the worries of blowouts. They are most effective when they slow down, calculate the risks, weigh the options, and receive wise counsel from others. Reflection and balance will protect them from their volatile emotions which can ignite their dynamite personalities.

The best way to relate to "D"s is straightforward. Don't beat around the bush. Get to the bottom line. They will certainly get to the bottom line with you! I once encouraged a fund raiser salesman who was going to meet with a high "D" school administrator to not waste his time. The salesperson was a high "I," and sometimes he talked too much. I advised him to get right to the point in his meeting. He told me later that he walked into the administrator's office and said, "Mels told me you're a high 'D', so here's what I can do for you." He took ten minutes and walked out with a $40,000 sale.

"D"s need choices. Parents and teachers of high "D" children need to harness their energy. Relate to them with respect for their ability to decide for themselves. Give them opportunities to be leaders. Don't stifle their drives. Point them in the right direction, give them parameters, and watch them fly!

These driven people are the best doers anywhere. They conquer life's greatest challenges, but unfortunately they seldom conquer themselves. When you think of steel and velvet, dominant people are characterized by steel, but they need to be sensitive to others. "D"s are drivers plowing their way through life, but they need to pave their way with pleasantness. Under the filling power of the Holy Spirit, they can be gentle and great for God's glory.

ENDNOTES

[1]Springle, Pat, *Trusting*, (Ann Arbor: Vine Books, 1994), pp. 115-116.

8

Calming The Inspiring Personality

I once underestimated the power of charisma, and in the process, I strained a good relationship. In the mid '80's, an elder in our church wanted to start a coffee house ministry. "Hootenannies" and coffee houses were no longer effective ministry vehicles for reaching young people, but my elder friend still thought it was a good idea.

He was an effective communicator. He and his wife were very popular in the church. She had a beautiful voice and he could also sing, and his gift was grassroots evangelism and discipleship. Our church was outreach-oriented, so he thought the coffee house idea would be a winner. When he brought it to the elder's meeting, I expressed my concerns because I felt he had a problem with pride. He wanted to be center stage at every church event, including our worship services.

I decided to talk to him about his pride, and to my amazement, he confessed his fault in one of our more heated elder's meetings. He placed himself on a temporary leave of absence. Later, when I learned more about personality types, I felt very guilty for the way I had treated him. I didn't understand the nature of his powerful personality, and I should have appreciated his abilities more. I should have encouraged him with his idea, or at least helped him shape it, but instead, I fought it.

I now realize that some people are born to shine. (Sometimes they even shine more than I do!) My responsibility is not to throw a blanket over their light. I need to help make their talents brighter! My ministry has been greatly blessed by understanding how certain people stand out above the rest.

Perhaps the easiest temperament to identify is the "I." They are the "Sparky Sanguines" of life. You'll find them leading, entertaining, and somehow adding to the positive atmosphere of every occasion.

"I"s are:
- Inspiring,
- Influencing,
- Interested in people,
- Impressive, and
- Inducing.

Naturally uninhibited, "I"s love to express themselves. They're the clowns of the class and the life of the party. Often raised in a family atmosphere that encouraged them to share their talents openly, "I"s are performers and people-pleasers. Their charisma and abilities to sway the crowd make them naturally persuasive speakers, salespersons, or actors.

Peter's Persuasion

The apostle Peter is a perfect illustration of an "I" type personality. Of all the New Testament leaders, Peter could best electrify the audience. Examine his famous sermon on the Day of Pentecost when three thousand souls were saved (Acts 2). Throughout the New Testament, he is found influencing people to follow Christ, however, Peter was fearful of a little maiden who questioned if he was one of the disciples (Matthew 26:73). In addition, Peter was challenged by Paul concerning his compromise of Jewish traditions.

One moment, Peter is inspired to follow Christ to the death and the next, he denies the Lord. One day Peter is excited about the kingdom, and the next, he quits the ministry to go back to fishing. Peter's up-and-down, on-and-off experiences are typical "I" behaviors. Peter is one of the most exciting and enthusiastic disciples, but he is also one of the most erratic. In the flesh, Peter was afraid of a little girl, but in the Spirit, Peter was fearful of no one. He seemed to evoke significant responses wherever he went. Peter was a great "salesperson," but sometimes he cared more about what others thought than what was right. As he matured in the faith and found his security and significance in Christ, he became a powerful preacher.

"I"s who work in sales positions sometimes have difficulty closing deals because they don't want to be rejected. A "No" is a blow to their pride. Although "I"s give the impression of high ego strength like "D"s, they are much more sensitive to being hurt and manipulated than their domineering counterparts. Their charisma and ability to communicate only gives the illusion of inner strength.

Inspiring, sensitive people in sales may be more concerned about making a good impression than selling the product. I once helped a furniture store owner interview a prospective salesperson. The lady was a high "I" with great selling ability. I wanted to teach her how strengths can become weaknesses, and how her communication skills could become her downfall. I said, "Let me prove something to you," then paused. There was a moment of silence.

She broke the silence with, "What are you trying to prove?"

And I said, "I just proved it." Then I paused again, even longer.

The silence was deafening, so she said anxiously, "I don't understand. What did you just prove?"

I said, "I just proved it again," then paused once more.

Obviously confused, she rattled, "This is scary! What did you just prove?"

I finally explained, "Every time I paused, you had to speak. You couldn't stand the silence. Good salespeople know when to talk and when to ask questions. The best salespeople are those who get customers to talk themselves into buying the product."

Happy Faces

"I"s want to bring others together to get results. They are active individuals who create positive environments for others. They are optimists, and they work best through people. One of their greatest strengths is the ability to relate to people; they are easily accepted and popular. They communicate well with others because they can use words and emotions effectively.

In 1984, Dr. Tim LaHaye arranged for me to be invited to a special briefing with President Ronald Reagan in the White House. The briefing focused on the American family and traditional values. I remember being in a elevator crowded with a group of preachers on board. The door closed and no one said a word. The seconds seemed like an eternity. Everyone wanted to say something, but we all waited for someone else to break the silence. Finally, one of the pastors said, "This is a great crowd for an offering." We all laughed and I thought to myself, "He's definitely an 'I.'"

"I"s are the people who make small talk in the checkout lines at supermarkets. While other shoppers look for the shortest or fastest lane, "I"s enjoy the opportunity to socialize with people. They like to help other shoppers in the store whether they work there or not. If someone looks confused, "I"s naturally respond, "Can I help you?" They enjoy making people feel good.

Cheerleaders At Heart

"I"s are cheerleaders. Even when they aren't up front, they stimulate those around them. They are natural spark plugs. They generate tremendous enthusiasm, and they entertain people. "I"s want to help others to feel good or accomplish a goal. They love to participate in groups where they can stand out. "I"s often take control of a group, not because of a strong desire to have their say, but because others won't. In order to avoid feeling uncomfortable, they naturally step out and lead.

These influencers prefer environments which include acceptance and social recognition. They are very friendly and enjoy back slapping, hugging, and encouraging others. They fill the air with laughter and joy.

King David demonstrated "I" behavior when he influenced people with his great charisma. God inspired David to write most of the Psalms. He was effective as a leader and speaker, but his weakness was selfishness and carnal interests. Able to entice Bathsheba into an adulterous relationship, David fell prey to sin. But there is another side to David's life. Because of David's sensitivity to God, he became an example to all who fall and get back up. Psalm 32 describes David's appreciation for God's forgiveness.

In Psalm 51:12-13, David asks God to restore the "joy of his salvation" so that he could teach others about God's grace and forgiveness. His depth of feeling is evident in this powerful, sensitive psalm. David was a "people person" with strong emotional drives.

Recognition is a strong incentive for "I"s. They desire the freedom of individual expression to win approval. Their unique ability to speak spontaneously about anything and everything often gains them recognition in crowds. They can be found in an abundance of group activities outside their jobs. Where there's a crowd, there's

an "I." Relaxing alone is not their style; they need and seek relationships. Because of their friendly demeanor, their interests are
often crowd-centered.

A recent experiment proved how persuasive "I"s can be. Several preschoolers where asked to lie about the taste of some juice
during snack time. They were told that the teacher's friend made
the juice and needed to be told how good it was. The juice tasted
terrible.

After sampling the juice all the children agreed it tasted terrible, but they promised to say it tasted good. When the teacher's
friend met each of the students individually, certain children could
not hide the fact that they didn't like it. They said the juice was
good, but their body language and nonverbal communication said
they were lying.

Other students, however, hid their feelings. They enthusias-
tically shared how much they liked the juice. Their open, bubbly,
high "I" personality covered up the truth. They were able to lie
convincingly about an unquestionable fact. Interestingly, the students who could lie without showing it were the ones who were
leaders during playtime. The students who couldn't hide their feelings became followers. Those who lied were more active and aggressive, and they spent most of playtime telling the passive, honest
kids what to do.

I'm obviously not advocating lying, but I am warning "I" personalities to be careful with reality. They must guard their persuasive personalities and always speak the truth.

Work Environment

"I"s will never be slaves to time. They don't like time controls
because they have trouble pulling themselves away from people.
The task at hand is never as important as the people with whom
they want to talk. Details are often seen as stumbling blocks. With

broad, sweeping, verbal strokes, "I"s can easily fly right over the nitty gritty, leaving details to others. They are concerned about new opportunities for recognition and acceptance, so opportunities to verbalize their proposals or ideas are very important to them.

Their strong need for favorable working conditions frustrates them when they are confronted with adversity. High "I"s need to concentrate on the task at hand. They are easily distracted, especially if they are working alone. "I"s are often tempted to help someone or just stop and talk rather than work productively alone. They need others who respect their sincerity. They tend to give confusing messages about themselves, and they are often misunderstood as being proud or cocky. In reality, they are very sensitive to what people think.

"I"s need to focus on the facts because many of their decisions are based on emotions. They need to learn to collect more information and consider all the options before coming to a conclusion.

Peter swore he would never deny the Lord, but his confidence and optimism short-circuited his ability to think clearly. Rebekah's enthusiasm to marry a man she had never seen in spite of her family's concern is characteristic of "I" behavior. They tend to jump into things; they make great initiators. Because they desire to talk so much, they often say whatever comes off the tops of their heads which may make them sound ambiguous and shallow. They should concentrate more on getting to the point and being specific.

Being surrounded by others with systematic approaches to problem-solving is very beneficial to these inspiring people. They need others who can deal with details and design the systems of follow-through to accomplish tasks. "I"s make "great ideas" employees. They can be extremely creative, but they need to focus on getting the job done. To be honest with you, I have started a million jobs and finished only a few. People say I'm creative, but I often wonder what they say about all my unfinished "great ideas." My wife and friends have really helped me focus. One of my favorite Bible verses is, "This one thing I do" (Phil 3:13). In the first half of my life, I concentrated on starting lots of new, innovative projects, but now in the last half of my life, I'm working harder on finishing well.

Strong Feelings

Because "I"s are primarily guided by feelings, they need to focus on the process of decision-making and individual follow-through. They are easily distracted and tend to be undisciplined and disorganized. Training themselves to sit and think on their own is an important step in their work habits. Instead of constantly seeking an ear to listen to them, they need to do more research in order to become more self-efficient.

"I"s need to practice taking a logical (rather than the social) approach to their problem-solving. They need to learn to demonstrate individual stick-to-it-ness. As promoters and persuaders, "I"s have the ability to spark interest and enthusiasm in others for just about anything. If, however, they lack the drive to see tasks through to completion, their energy and power of persuasion are wasted. They should constantly strive to perfect their follow-through and complete what they've started. Organizational skills to help them manage their tasks include clock watching, scheduling, and personal planning.

Some "I" children are misunderstood by their parents. These excitable, enthusiastic kids may be tagged "hyperactive," but in reality, they are only being themselves. Parents of "I" children need to give a lot of positive strokes because these kids need more approval and recognition than others. (Keep in mind, all children respond best to affirming, optimistic influences.) Pessimistic parents can be very discouraging to these sensitive children. Interactive parents make great encouragers, but poor examples. "I"s tend to be too dramatic, and as parents, they can be "screamers." Their overly expressive behavior makes "I" children reactive. "I" parents need to learn to control their emotions and be calm. Children learn how to react by watching their parents, so screaming parents usually produce screaming kids.

"I"s need to control their time more wisely. They are often defeated by the clock, overwhelmed by the pressure of schedules and deadlines because they naturally mismanage their time. They should realize that there isn't time for everyone and everything in the day. Thinking ahead and planning for interruptions are practical steps. Because they talk so much, they usually take a lot of time to complete tasks, so they should give themselves more leeway. It is wise for them to set time limits and schedule earlier deadlines. Talking does not always solve problems and accomplish tasks. In fact, conversation often prolongs a project. In order to be productive, "I"s must learn the value of solitude and silence. Those who plan time alone can better manage their natural ability to interact with others. Also, they should respect the time restrictions of other people's schedules. Silence is an important commodity for these gregarious people to acquire. They will become more objective if they think before expressing themselves. They should consider the amount of time and thought they have given a matter before coming to any conclusions. "I"s should weigh their words wisely before speaking. Although they tend to get away with things because they're popular, they should strive to be "slow to speak and quick to listen." They can avoid "me-firstitis" by going out of their way to include people in discussions and decision-making. Learning to let others speak for themselves is essential, and allowing others to share in the "limelight" forces them to take a back seat.

Because of their confidence and uninhibited personalities, "I"s tend to think more highly of themselves than of others. A more realistic appraisal of their associates can be humbling. Letting others go first and sharing the spotlight minimizes the possibility that they will be criticized for pride.

Competing Partners

"I" spouses tend to be too communicative, and they can be too sensitive about feelings. "I"s often want to know what their mates are thinking, but they seldom wait for answers. When a person tries to express himself, they interrupt and never let him finish. "I"s need to be patient and focus on the other person. They also need to be careful not to concentrate on what they're going to say as soon as the person pauses to take a breath.

I know of a couple who have enough "I" in them that their conversations tend to get exciting. They're both very expressive! A friend dropped in on them while they were in the middle of one of their verbal battles. Since they're all good friends, they decided to share with the one who dropped by the husbands frustrations about his wife's picky perfectionism. She interrupted and clarified every other sentence. He also interrupted and heard little of what she said.

He overreacted and got angry! She eventually left the room crying. Their poor friend never expected this! It's one of the few times in many years of marriage that they ever had a spat in public, but the husband learned a tremendous lesson. Their friend observed that neither of them listened to the other because they were so intent on talking. They'll never forget their friend's timely advice: Once your feelings are shared, ask the person listening to repeat what he or she heard. What the husband says is often not what the wife hears. We're all responsible for making what we say clear. It is never the wife's fault for not hearing the husband correctly. Since the day their friend showed them how to communicate better, the husband has often said, "I'm so sorry I didn't make myself clear. Let me try again."

This perspective works a lot better than accusing the other for not listening! Don't criticize your mate for not hearing what you are saying. I often say in training seminars, "The teacher hasn't taught until the students have learned."

"I" partners compete for the air waves, and they can also compete for attention. Two "I"s in a marriage or working relationship can become jealous of each other. They must learn to appreciate one another's talents and be willing to learn from each other rather than constantly tell the other what to do. They sincerely want to express themselves, but they need to remember that the other person may have the same desire. A little understanding and a lot of patience can go a long way with two "I"s. They demonstrate maturity and love when they allow someone else to have center stage.

Because "I"s are sensitive, they tend to avoid offending people. They need to learn that being firm and honest can be more important to others than being friendly. They have a keen sense of the mood of groups of people. This makes them natural leaders with the ability to inspire and influence people. Their friendliness is a blessing at every function.

Sources of Conflict

"I"s over-promise and under-deliver. Desiring to please everyone, they build high expectations, and people are often disappointed by their unfulfilled promises. When asked to do something, it's better to respond, "I'll rather let you know than to let you down. Let me get back to you about whether I can do what you ask."

They also struggle when they don't get the credit or attention they deserve. If they feel overlooked, they can be very expressive about their disappointment. They need to remember, God made them like a mirror to reflect His glory, not theirs.

They may irritate others by talking too much, not being on time, and being disorganized. Conflicts often arise with those who are more task-oriented, but "I"s usually relate well to people-oriented people. They make great first impressions but must work to avoid conflicts because of irresponsibility and the appearance of laziness. Also, they need to control their feelings and make decisions based on reason.

Emotionally, "I"s tend to experience extreme highs and lows. The "downs" typically don't last long, however, and they return to their optimism. They also tend to wear their feelings on their sleeves. They may discover that it is beneficial at times to keep their feelings to themselves and wait for the right time to express them. Their enthusiastic and exciting personalities make others glad to know them. Life would be boring without "I"s.

Relating To Relational Types

These influential people are extremely relational, but sometimes they are too "touchy feely." They respond best to those who allow them to express their feelings. They need genuine complements; don't flatter them. Recognize their beauty and talents, and try to reinforce positive character traits as well as their accomplishments. Allow them to shine and share. Don't stifle their creativity or pull the plug on their energy, but encourage them to use their abilities for Christ. They need to guard against their desire for honor and recognition.. "I"s can become persuasive leaders, but they need to remember to please the Lord, not just people.

9

Stimulating The Shy Personality

The highest percentage of people fall into the category of the passive, people-oriented type of personality. They are shy and reserved, but they often make the best friends and most loyal employees.

Perhaps you've heard of individuals who took the blame for things they didn't do. They willingly accepted punishment, even though they were not guilty. History has given us many lessons of those who suffered for the sins of others. The best example is how Jesus suffered for everyone's wrongs though He was faultless. His love motivated Him to live and die for others. Loyalty motivates some people to suffer for the wrongs of others. They would rather endure pain themselves than to allow others to hurt. This can be a wonderful quality, but it can also be a dangerous fault.

I've seen my wife, who is so loving and sacrificing, give of herself, rather than let anyone down. She's always willing to help others, regardless how she might feel. Her personality is sweet and sensitive, and everyone loves her. She has an "S" type personality.

"S"s are:

• Stable,
• Steady,
• Security-oriented, and
• Sensitive.

"S"s emphasize cooperating with others to carry out tasks. They are submissive servants who usually end up doing what the "D" has dreamed and "I" promoted. "S"s are soft hearted and sensitive. They may be seen as timid, but they are tireless in their labor. They let others lead, they avoid conflicts, and they strive for the status quo. Change is difficult for them, so innovation and creativity are left to others.

These people prefer sitting or staying in a single place. Their passiveness is often perceived as laziness by extroverts, but they are steady work horses. They quietly get the job done while others push, talk, play, or criticize. "S"s don't like to make waves. Instead, they work to calm them, creating stability and security around them. Tranquility in the midst of turmoil is their specialty. Their staying power is incredible. While others lose their patience, nothing seems to unravel these steady, reliable people. They seldom openly show their feelings, and if they do, they quietly cry or laugh to themselves. Patience is more than a voluntary virtue; it's a way of life for them.

Moses went from "hero to zero"—from being the son of Pharaoh's daughter to the backside of the desert. His self-esteem went from the pinnacle to the pits. Moses came to the place in his life where he learned God's sufficiency. His "S" type personality is seen when he was commanded by God to lead the children of Israel out of Egypt, but he resisted this responsibility. He felt insecure, unstable, and unsure of himself. Moses even suggested to God that Aaron be the leader because Aaron was a better speaker. In typical "S" fashion, Moses would rather let Aaron be up front and in charge. Moses, however, learned that God was his strength. God was his security and stability. In the flesh, Moses was shy, but in the Spirit, he was strong.

"S"s are extremely loyal, and they often work with the same company for years. They also tend to be family-oriented and dedicated to their loved ones. Interest in their families is evident by the photos and mementos covering their walls or desks.

Abraham showed "S" type behavior in his strong family ties. He was a good listener and friend, and he trusted of God in spite of difficulties. He was steady and stable in the midst of uncertainty.

"S"s don't like aggression or antagonism. Their strong sense of loyalty, however, compels them to come to the aid of family or friends who are in trouble. They ardently defend them physically and verbally, stepping out of their comfort zone, shocking themselves and others.

They aren't interested in showing off in a large group. They tend to seek out personal relationships, talking one-on-one or to a few people at a time. "S"s have the ability to listen for hours about anything. They are "people-people" with the ability to work while they talk or listen.

Calm In The Storm

Athletics brings out the best and worst in people. Tom Landry, former head football coach of the Dallas Cowboys, gives us a lesson in control. I never saw him lose his temper. In fact, the most expressive thing I ever saw him do was extend his arm with a closed fist and whisper, "All right!" after a Super Bowl touchdown. On the other hand, John Madden, former coach of the L. A. Raiders, would run up and down the sideline demonstrating his feelings.

Athletes express their personalities in different ways. "D" football players knock your block off and then growl in your face. "I" players are the ones who invented the end zone dance. (My favorite to watch is "Neon Deon" Sanders .) "S" athletes may knock you silly, but then say they're sorry. "C"s ask lots of questions and execute best when they know exactly what to do.

Competitive sports create elation, pressures, and roller coaster rides in short periods of time. "S"s seem to handle the challenge better than anyone. Sometimes they handle it too well, and they don't get excited enough.

Calming excited people and making others feel comfortable seems to come naturally to "S"s. They aren't high strung, and they usually make great marriage partners and employees because of their concern for a steady and stable environment. They respond calmly to aggression, often defusing problems with their sincere interest and self-controlled temperament. They seek cooperation rather than control. As peacemakers, "S"s are servants who work patiently and persistently to resolve conflicts between people.

Because they have the patience to develop specialized skills, they often learn skills others won't or can't learn. "S"s appreciate routine rather than despise it. Their ability to do the same thing repeatedly makes them specialists. Concentrating on the task at hand is a great strength. They don't become easily bored because of their ability to concentrate on getting the job done. Their attitude of persistent service makes them invaluable to employers.

"S"s want high touch, not high tech. They want to support and serve, maintaining the status quo routine because they feel insecure with change. New things, especially high tech things, are threatening to them. They work best under controlled, stable environments. IBM concluded that business owners and managers needed to upgrade their equipment for faster and more efficient productivity, but "S" secretaries resisted. Therefore, IBM designed a commercial that said, "It's okay to get a new typewriter as long as it's an IBM."

"S"s usually don't make a big deal about anything. They do their work well without fanfare. Sincere appreciation and consistency make them happy because they desire an environment which includes security. Safety is imperative, and they shudder at the thought that someone could possibly get hurt. To these safety conscious people, security is the positive product of happy and healthy surroundings.

Don't rearrange the office furniture without giving "S"s ample time to evaluate. They need explanation for changes, and they want time to adapt. They prefer slow alterations and easy turnovers. They like to create stability in their environment . . . and to preserve that stability.

One of the most important environments to preserve is the home environment. "S"s require minimal work infringement on their home life. They desire 9:00 to 5:00 work schedules, and they want their weekends to be free.

Appreciation Means Everything

I have known many "S"s who generously gave themselves to others. A pastor friend served his church for years. The church had grown slowly but solidly. He had sacrificed his rest, study time, and sometimes his family's needs for the sake of his members. After years of his tireless service, one deacon became antagonistic toward him. This deacon was a "D" who wanted to see more action and growth. "D"s can be every pastor's dream or nightmare. In this case, the deacon became defiant and disloyal. Eventually the conflict was more than the pastor could stand, so for the sake of his church, the pastor made the ultimate sacrifice and resigned. For him, flight was better than fight.

If the church had been more appreciative of his labor of love, he may have stayed. However, he felt like the church didn't appreciate him. "S"s desire credit for the work they do, but they seldom express that need. Although they accomplish many tasks, "S"s are often the unsung heroes. A little credit where credit is due goes a long way with them. They don't get excited about red stars next to their names. They need simple, sincere appreciation. They lack high ego strengths, so they often appear to have low self-esteem, and their quiet demeanor is often misunderstood. Their strength is quietly and methodically seeing a job through to completion. "S"s often seek identification with a group. They don't want to dominate or direct, but they need to be a part of a team. Of course, they tend to become active in serving others, but they also relish the opportunity to develop potential friendships. Their slow responses to pressure makes them an asset to any group. "S"s are not self-promoting, though they are self-protective.

In a crowd, they're the silent crusaders. They need leaders who will speak up for them and take up their causes, especially when they are discouraged. "S"s desire someone to defend their feelings and promote their needs—someone to be assertive for them.

Jacob demonstrated "S" behavior when he stayed at the job of creating a better breeding method to increase his herd. He was manipulated by Laban and his brother Esau, but Jacob persisted and eventually got what he wanted. He wrestled with God. He worked fourteen years to get his wife. While most men would have quit, Jacob persisted.

Satisfied With The Status-Quo

Detailed procedures are important to "S"s, and they prefer environments where they can consistently operate without confusion. Because of their need for security, they desire limited territory. Familiar, comfortable surroundings give them more confidence. Their sense of comfort comes from predictable patterns and familiar situations. They often withdraw from new challenges to avoid the risk of failure, and they are usually slow to speak and appear less active than others. They feel most comfortable with standardized procedures. Without this standardization and simplicity, they may become unsettled and insecure.

"S"s need more organization than explanation. Once procedures are clarified, they can follow them better than the extroverts. They even enjoy the simple tasks that often frustrate others, but everything must be explained and organized for them in a simple and understandable manner.

They need exposure to people who react quickly to the unexpected. Because of their slow responses, they need to build relationships with those who can handle sudden challenges well. By understanding their own apprehension about change, "S"s can adapt to a situation more easily. Reacting quickly is sometimes just as important as reacting smoothly, therefore they can benefit by observing those who respond more quickly to opportunities or difficulties.

"S"s should stretch themselves to meet the challenges of an unexpected task. Their need for stability should not stifle opportunities to serve others. Though they are uncomfortable with change, they can respond to unexpected situations if they understand their natural reluctance. To stretch themselves, they should become involved in more than one thing at a time, not allowing their insecurity in a situation to cause them to withdraw. They are capable of many tasks with the proper scheduling of time and space.

Supervising "S"s should include constant reinforcement. They usually prefer for others to take on new jobs and challenges, but they need to realize their own capabilities and have confidence to tackle new opportunities. They probably can do a lot more by exerting a little more confidence.

Lean On Me

Known as "Flip Phlegmatics," "S"s tend to flip back and forth according to the amount of pressure put on them. Their easygoing nature is so flexible that they may give the impression of having no convictions or strong emotions. Since they seldom respond outwardly to pressure, they provide a welcome balance to bold, outspoken people. They need to become more assertive in unpredictable circumstances.

Barnabas could influence the crowd and encourage individuals. His "S" behavior is seen in his support of John Mark. Some people may see Barnabas as a compromiser, but perhaps he should be viewed as a peace maker. His gentle demeanor and good report of Paul, in spite of their conflict, is typical of an "S." Barnabas didn't like conflict. He even avoided fellowship with Gentiles so he would not offend his Jewish friends.

"S"s need to be more assertive and less sensitive. Rather than avoid confrontation, they should learn to respond more assertively. They need to overcome their fear of being intimidated by others.

Since many people are "S"s, situations often arise where there are *all Indians and no chief.* When a need arises, someone must take responsibility and assume leadership. Someone needs to become decisive rather than quietly waiting for other people to respond.

The "S"s' greatest weakness is being naive. They have trouble saying, "No!" Everyone knows they will do what no one else wants to do because they care so much about pleasing others.

I personally admire "S" behavior the most because it happens to be my greatest need. I respect their ability to stay calm. Unfortunately, their slow response and laissez faire attitude are often misunderstood as laziness or lack of commitment. They can be misunderstood as wishy washy, but their loyalty and calm are great strengths. My hat's off to "S"s! May their tribe increase!

"S"s, however, can be doormats for aggressive, insensitive people. If you're an "S" and live or work with someone who abuses you sexually, physically, emotionally, or verbally, I strongly encourage you to get professional help. You must learn how to be strong for yourself! Talk to your minister or a counselor, but don't just wish the problem away. It won't go away until you do something about it. Whatever you do, don't try to solve it overnight. You can't just put your foot down and demand that things change. Significant change takes time, planning, and courage.

Assertiveness training courses can help you. Recognize the fact that your best attribute can potentially become your worst liability. Beware that the strength of being a servant does not become the weakness of subservience. Your desire to serve will generally be supervised by a strong person, but don't let them take advantage of you.

"S"s enjoy relationships with people who contribute to the task at hand. Though they are willing to do it all themselves, they work best as part of a team. Getting input from others adds security to their environment. They are prone to become caught up in conversation and neglect their work, but they are also willing to work all night to accomplish a job, especially if someone else will work with them.

"S"s need co-workers who are flexible in their work procedures. Bosses may demand the task be done their way, but these people often feel that they work better alone and without pressure. They are comfortable when doing the job at their own pace, and others would be wise to give them some flexibility. However, they need to learn to adapt to changing situations. Conditioning them to change increases their productivity. Sometimes the rules change halfway through the game, but that doesn't mean it's time to stop or slow down.

"S"s must learn to respond more quickly to pressure and be more assertive. The impatience of others bothers them. They are patient themselves, and not quickly frustrated. They feel pressure when instant change is demanded. Immediate action is threatening to them.

Because they believe that others can accomplish tasks faster or better, "S"s need continual reassurance that their contributions are invaluable. Communicating specific, sincere praise to them is imperative because they want to know their work and service are appreciated.

Sources of Conflict

"S"s avoid conflict better than anyone, but they can act just like "D"s when you mess with their family or friends! They can be extremely protective, and they often take up other people's offensives. Like a mother hen, "S"s can attack and react with surprising force. Submissive people resist pushy and bossy people, and they respond best to those who are steady and security-oriented. They don't like challenges. "S"s get nervous when things get hot. Sometimes their craving for stability can make them unstable, and they explode or do crazy things when they are overcome with pressure.

On television, we sometimes see news accounts about employees who have been fired and then return to murder the boss, employees, and even customers. They couldn't take the stress. Their world crumbles, then they snap. People wonder, "He was such a quiet guy. I can't believe he would ever do such a thing." "S"s are not the only ones capable of crazy behavior. All people have their buttons and emotional pressure points. When pressed too hard, anyone can break. "S"s, however, repress their feelings. Other personalities seem to be able to express and resolve their emotions better than these security conscious people.

"S"s are irritated by people who are disloyal. They work hard for those who are appreciative and kind to them. They don't seek lots of friends, but they will be faithful to those who prove to be trustworthy. I've seen "S" ladies who wouldn't hurt a flea become strong leaders when their families were threatened. I once saw a quiet, reserved mother become a "maniac on a mission" when the school principle verbally condemned her son. She confronted him with fire on her breath! She held nothing back. Her power took everyone by surprise. Afterwards, she was apologetic for her outrage, but she didn't need to be. Her response accomplished precisely what she intended, and she got her message across with authority. "S"s can bite your head off, then say they're sorry later. God uses them in great ways, but they often doubt their influence.

The Power Of Relationships

"S" make great parents, teachers, mates, employees, and friends, but they need to be more sure of themselves. Assertiveness training can be helpful, but be wary of secular assertiveness training. The world emphasizes, "I'm # 1." Secular assertiveness training is self-centered, but we need the be God-centered. "S"s who desire to be more assertive may benefit from finding a godly, successful businessperson in their church who will mentor them. "S"s may not be aggressive enough to ask someone for help, but one of the most important things they can do is to ask someone help them be more assertive.

I once counseled a couple who both had high "S" personalities. Their sixteen year old daughter was a "D" who threatened to run away if her parents didn't let her do what she wanted. The child had control of the family. In fact, the roles were reversed: The parents acted like children, and the child acted like the parent. I encouraged the parents to be more firm. Don't give "D" teens an ultimatum such as, "If you don't like it, there's the door!" They will chose the door and devastate the "S" parents. Instead, give the child choices, and give her opportunities to be responsible. Gradually let the child assume greater responsibility for her choices as she matures. "S"s don't want conflict so they usually give in to the child's demands, so design a compromise that shows your willingness to trust and your determination still to be in control. I know it's not as easy as it sounds, but carefully consider how your personality affects your relationships.

Supervising and confronting "S"s at work is much like dealing with family members. They respond best to leaders who are understanding and friendly. They don't like antagonistic environments. Appreciative relationships with others make them feel good about their work environment. Their effectiveness can be increased by working with those of equal competence. They become angry and stifled when superiors constantly correct them. Working with equals with similar attitudes and abilities makes them more productive.

Give "S"s guidelines for accomplishing a task. As faithful friends and loyal workers, they don't always ask questions. Instead, they make assumptions in order to work quietly on their own. Provide specific directions to enable them to feel secure about the tasks they are accomplishing. Encourage their creativity. Force them to "step out" of their shells and try something new and daring. Creativity may not come easily for people who would rather follow a prescribed ritual at home or at work, but wonderful experiences and victories are theirs once they learn to be more imaginative.

As natural skeptics, "S"s should strive to be more positive and persuasive. Their demands for safety and security may seem petty and demanding to others. This need for stability discourages them from assertive, risk-taking roles.

"S"s should remember that a lack of friction is not always positive. Pleasing others sometimes is a defense, not a strength. Of all the temperaments, however, people with this temperament will have the fewest enemies and the longest history of effective service.

Esther was very loyal to her people. She showed "S" behavior by being willing to die. She stated bravely, "If I perish, I perish" (Esther 4:16). She was also very creative. Her tendency toward pessimism was overcome by her faith in God's providential care. Esther was willing to die for what she believed. She let God turn her natural weakness into a supernatural strength. Her commitment seemed uncharacteristic of "S"s. She was naturally timid and shy, but in the power of the Holy Spirit she responded in a strong way. Her intense love and loyalty made her stand firm, and she was an example to everyone who fears conflict.

2 Corinthians 12:10 teaches when we are weak, God can be strong in us. As long as we rely on our natural strengths, we will not think we need help, or perhaps we think we are so weak that no one can help us. When we realize we cannot do something, then we can trust in God and draw on His strength. "S"s' dependency makes them powerful servants in the hands of a mighty God.

Relating To "S"s

"S" respond best to warmth and friendliness. They don't like to be pushed into anything, so give them time to change. They make wonderful Sunday school teachers, but don't change their room or curriculum half way through the quarter!

They are slow to make friends because they don't initiate relationships. They listen well, but you have to ask them questions to get them to talk. Show genuine interest in their family and friends; be patient and kind. Try to see life as they do, and you will probably enjoy life more. Learn from them; relax; don't attack people; don't fight back; slow down and smell the roses.

Life is more simple to "S"s, but they aren't simple people. They may be very talented, but you may never know it because they don't like to show off. Encourage them to share their talents in a small group before asking them to perform in front of a large crowd.

"S"s can have great testimonies, but they seldom share them. They feel people aren't really interested, or they think they can't communicate their stories well enough. A friend once shared her testimony to a small group of ladies. She was extremely shy. Just thinking about doing it just about killed her! Other people can't understand how difficult public speaking can be for others. She felt like she was going to die! She sheepishly shared how God had worked in her life, and everyone was encouraged by her message. She was relieved once it was over. (Her heart started beating again!) God began to use this unwilling and fragile servant in a mighty way. People overlooked her fear and saw how real Jesus was to her.

"S"s can have powerful ministries once they get past their shyness. They make wonderful friends in times of crisis. God uses "S"s in mighty ways when they allow His power to flow through them.

10

Satisfying the Cautious Personality

I know someone who is never wrong! She is right about just about everything. Every time she is wrong I sing the doxology, but I'm beginning to forget the words because I sing it so seldom!

Sometimes she irritates the stew out of me! Once I had enough of her nitpicking, so I confronted her, "You're too pessimistic!"

"I'm not pessimistic," she responded. "I'm realistic."

I thought that was clever, but it was only an excuse for her constant questioning and analysis of everything anyone ever said or did! I also told her, "You worry too much, too!"

She replied calmly, "I don't worry. I just get concerned."

She probably worries (or "gets concerned") too much. "D"s don't worry enough, and it sometimes gets them into trouble. We often take too many risks, but "C"s carefully analyzes things before they take any risk at all.

"C"s are:
- Calculating,
- Conservative,
- Cautious,
- Competent, and
- Compliant.

"C"s promote quality in products or services in existing circumstances. They are task-oriented, passive people. As thinkers and analyzers, they work on solving problems. High tech is more important than high touch to them. They respond to form and function rather than feelings, therefore reasoning rather than relationship drives them.

"C"s pursue perfection and sometimes carry correctness to extremes. They prefer to accomplish one thing correctly than to partially complete ten tasks. They follow directions and standards very carefully, and they want to comply with the rules while stressing quality in their work. They have very high standards, and they concentrate on details. They want to do everything "just right."

"C" teachers may have the most attractive bulletin boards in the entire school, but when they are complemented, they respond, "But look at the upper left hand border. It's a quarter of an inch off!" These picky people pinpoint problems rather than focus on the potential. They are more aware of burdens than blessings. "D"s would say, "Who cares? You got the bulletin board done." "I"s would probably want to borrow it for them to use next quarter. And an "S"s would politely ask, "I helped put it up. Can I help you, too?"

Doubting Thomas

A good example of "C" behavior is Thomas, the disciple. Though he has the reputation of being a doubter, he was obviously a competent and cautious follower of Christ. He was more consistent than

Peter. Historians write that Thomas and his disciples were fervent missionaries to India. He became a doer instead of a doubter. In the flesh, Thomas would not believe until he saw the nail-scarred hands of the risen Savior, but in the Spirit, Thomas became a great evangelist. Thomas needed proof, but when the confusion was cleared, he was a real powerhouse for the Lord. As a "C", Thomas questioned the unknown. He was not going to jump into anything, but when Jesus walked through the door to the upper room without even opening it and showed His hands and side, Thomas fell to his knees and cried, "My Lord and my God, (John 20:28)." Thomas didn't need to feel the scars in Christ's hands or touch the hole in His side. He was convinced by looking.

"C"s are not easy believers. They need explanations and answers. They often have to analyze the problems before exercising their faith. They work well in controlled environments. They tend to be conservative decision-makers, checking all the options and leaving no loose ends. They need precision and predictability.

"C"s are diplomatic with most people, but they can also be critical. Weighing their words for effectiveness, they may inflict vicious verbal jabs to make their point. Correctness is the their greatest concern. They constantly check for accuracy. They tend to be quite competent, but they are only cautiously confident. Accepting a fact at face value is very difficult because they feel compelled to dig deeper or probe further. This analyzing can be annoying for others, but in most cases their thoroughness is reassuring. Because they aren't satisfied with surface answers, these calculating people turn over every leaf and read every line. Their inquisitive natures consume them. They need in-depth answers.

Methodical

The apostle Luke was obviously a "C." He was meticulous in the details of his gospel and the Book of Acts. A physician by training, Luke was an objective thinker. He methodically approached life as a tactician. Luke's writings are concise and clear; he concentrated on specific facts. He cared about details rather than receiving credit for what he did or who he was. His dedication to the Lord and his bent toward accuracy made him a valued disciple and historian.

"C"s tend to become experts in specific areas because they absorb themselves in whatever they do. They criticize freely, no matter if it is their performance or another person's. Seldom is anything ever 100% right in the their eyes. With an eye for quality, they strive to better themselves and others. Finding a better way of doing things is their cup of tea.

They are critical thinkers. They ask, "Why?" and tell you if something could be done better. At times, precise thinking makes them too picky. They can be thorns in the flesh because they are naturally pessimistic and find flaws.

As passive individuals, "C"s tend to comply with authority. They are not aggressive when confronted with a challenge. Instead, they try to find a way to fix the problem. They don't desire to be in control for control's sake, but they demand that things be done correctly and in order. They don't respond well to differences. Complying is easier for them than communicating, and they believe silent surrender is better than open confrontation. However, this often leads them to hold grudges, engraving in granite the memories of past offenses. Forgiving and forgetting are very difficult for them. Known as "Moody Melancholies," they tend to drown themselves in introspective reflection rather than engage in open communication.

Because they question everything, including themselves, these critical, calculating people need to be continually reassured. They focus on problems rather than solutions, and this challenge demands they work in sheltered, stable conditions. The slightest trouble is magnified in their minds, and dealing with more than one problem at a time can be overwhelming for them. "C"s need constant encouragement because they are pessimistic by nature. Their concern for correctness causes them to worry. They seem to doubt more than most.

Job had friends who demonstrated Murphy's Law long before anyone ever heard of Murphy! They thought the worst. Job's so-called friends jumped to conclusions, judging and condemning him.

Faith and optimism are often foreign to them. It's hard for them to relax when problems exist all around them. Their theme song could easily be Hee Haw's popular tune, "Gloom, despair, agony on me. Deep, dark depression, excessive misery. If it weren't for bad luck, I'd have no luck at all. Gloom, despair and agony on me." Instead, "C"s would do well to sing, "Don't worry! Be happy!"

The need to prove their competence can cause conflicts. I have a friend whose "D" personality clashes with his wife's "C." Sometimes he comes home with a brilliant idea. He wants his wife to bow down and say, "That's a terrific idea! You're so smart! Go for it! Do it!" He'll begin to present his thoughts, but halfway through she finds three things wrong with his idea. (He's lucky she stopped at three!) Her response never fails to take the wind right out of his sails. He has trouble dealing with it, but actually, he needs her analysis and caution to balance his enthusiasm.

Interestingly, the problems his wife sees are usually very important issues which he needs to consider, and he's embarrassed because he didn't think about them first. He once got upset and said, "Why do you have to be so negative? Why do you have to be so fault-finding?"

And she responds, "Why do you have to be so stupid? Why didn't you see those problems first?"

She's the best thing that's ever happened to him. She forces him to raise his "C" and lower his "D," to think through his exciting ideas and bring them down to earth. Another time he got so angry he said, "You make me so mad I could bite your ear off."

She responded, "If you did, you'd have more brains in stomach than you do in your head."

He decided to keep his mouth shut!

Quality Control

"C"s want SOPs, standard operating procedures. They dislike uncertainty and want to know exactly when, why, how, where, and what. They are most comfortable when order is valued and confusion is limited. They work best under structured conditions, so consistency is critical. Abrupt alterations threaten them with their biggest emotional challenge: the fear of being incompetent. They think change for no good reason is insane. Others may scurry to test a new possibility, but "C"s drag their feet until convincing facts are presented.

The status quo allows them to refine and improve the system. "Quality control" is their personal motto. If they can't do it right, they don't want to do it at all. They are the perfect fit for the job that requires precision and detail. Because they are never satisfied unless they complete the job right, they are the consumers best friend because they sincerely desire to do the best job they can.

"C"s take great pride in their work. They are their own worst critics, but they appreciate recognition of their craftsmanship. They don't seek personal praise, but they appreciate attention for their finished product. You may criticize them, but don't criticize their work! "I"s are very sensitive to personal criticism, but they may not care if someone criticizes their performance. "C"'s are just the opposite. They take personal rebuke lightly, but are deeply offended if people dare to criticize their work! They enjoy situations that call attention to their accomplishments. They strive to provide first class products and services, and they prefer opportunities that focus on their projects rather than themselves.

"C"s usually want others to be in charge. Though they are often critical of leadership, they to need those who have final authority to make decisions. Willing and able to give direction, they often hesitate because of their cautious style. These cautious individuals seldom make mistakes because they seldom make decisions! "C"s who work closely with those in authority offer excellent counsel because they know they will not be ultimately responsible. This often gives them the freedom to be bolder than others.

Focused On The Function

"C"'s want to work on solving a particular problem, and they crave the chance to do what others can't do. Typically, they are slow decision-makers, and they can learn from decisive individuals. Instead of wishing they had more time, space, or money to do a better job, they should consider the counsel of superiors and then move ahead. They need to remember that expediency and sufficiency are sometimes best even if it means the quality of the work is a little less than perfect.

"C"s need supervisors who use policies as guidelines, not as threats. Giving them the flexibility and minimal restraints produces maximum results in their work. Limitations may be necessary, however, and they should be open for specific improvements. They want guidance, but they also want the opportunity to do things right.

They often give the impression of being so busy that people feel they can't get close to them. They become more and more disinterested in people as they are absorbed in their projects. Distractions annoy them and produce caustic responses. Written across their faces is, "Don't bother me, I'm busy!"

The prophet Elijah set up tests to prove which prophets truly represented God. He didn't tolerate hypocrisy or error, and he confronted Queen Jezebel's prophets. His job as a true prophet was serious business, and he became discouraged easily. He was susceptible to depression. When Jezebel threatened him, he fled and prayed for God to take his life. In this time of self-condemnation, Elijah learned to experience God's love and care.

"C"s are often fussy, but the motivation to look for flaws may be the desire to be superior to everyone else. They are often insensitive to the needs of the people closest to them. Unaware of other people's interests, they seem to drift into "Never Never Land." While searching for a better way, they can lose sight of reality.

My wife asks me questions like, "Why do we park on driveways and drive on parkways? Why is there a permanent press setting on my iron? Why is there an expiration date on sour cream? And why is the Secretary of the Interior involved with everything outdoors?"

My answer is, "I really don't know." And to tell the truth, I really don't care! Understanding the oddities in life are not important to me, but she is perceptive enough to see the inconsistencies in even the little things in life.

In Search Of Excellence

"C"s aren't adventurous, but they are inquisitive for quality's sake. Searching for new thrills is not nearly as important as seeking new truth. They need the balance provided by those who will compromise, and they need others to help them find the medium between opposing views. Often unwilling to compromise, they tend to offend others. Because of their natural ability to see problems, they should be careful about open criticism. They need to allow opportunities for others to state their positions. They would be wise to hold back at times and allow someone else to find flaws and make the first response so they aren't perceived as "always negative."

Precise, detail work allows them to be most effective, so they should look for jobs that require them to do what they do best. Working in a supportive environment with broad limitations and specific goals adds to their productivity. They need opportunities for careful planning. Their clarity and objectivity go hand-in-hand. Having time to think, evaluate, and make corrections is important. They deplore disorganization and carelessness. They prefer specific job descriptions, and they like to know exactly what their job requires. Without this clarity, confusion reigns and frustration results.

"C"s have an intense need to feel understood. When my oldest son, Curtis, was five years old, he asked me where God came from. I proceeded to expound: "God is preexistent. He has a quality of life that demands no beginning and no end. He is the Alpha and Omega, the First and the Last, the Almighty and Infinite One." After that scholarly dissertation, my son surprisingly responded, "Oh!" I'm sure he was thinking of ten other questions!

Because of their need for explanation, periodic appraisals should be scheduled. They desire feedback and help along the way, and evaluations of their performance from time to time enhances their work. They must learn to respect people as much as they respect their own accomplishments. Because of their strong task-orientation, they tend to get over-involved in projects and forget people, but the value of a person exceeds a completed project.

Developing tolerance for conflict is also a very important lesson for cautious, compliant "C"s. Their passive personalities cause them to withdraw and verbally hold back. They tend to run away in order to avoid trouble.

Because they are perceived as competent, they often get nominated for committees in the church. People know they don't make quick decisions; they are cautious and careful. I once went to a finance committee meeting with a gravy stained napkin with notes of what I wanted the church to do the next year. My friend, Cal

Robbins, shared later how the gravy stained napkin didn't impress him, especially when he noticed the gravy wasn't dry! He said, "You just jotted those notes at your dinner table before the meeting." He's a "C" and likes to see feasibility studies and validation reports. He was the VP of Human Resources of a large chain of department stores. He was a very effective board member; he definitely was not a "yes man," and I respected his judgment and insights.

From that experience, I learned that board members look at my plans through their unique personality perspectives. "D"s want me to get to the point. They like to see the bottom line. Short and decisive meetings are best. "I"s like to talk a lot and want opportunities to share their feelings. They're very sensitive to the emotional atmosphere in the church. "S"s are conscious of everyone's personal needs. They are very sensitive to the poor and needy, and they like to see love expressed in God's family. "C"s are the protectors of the faith. They scrutinize everything and guard every penny. They're a pain to an aggressive, visionary pastor!

I recommend pastors go to board meetings prepared to communicate to every personality type. "D"s respect strong leadership. Have a dream. Be purpose-driven. Set goals. "I"s are impressed with your optimism. Be positive and expressive. Show them you feel strongly about your proposals. "S"s are family-oriented. They're loyal. Be kind and patient. Treat them like you would want someone to treat your mother. Be gentle. "C"s need lots of explanation and time to change. They need for you to do your homework before you present an idea or plan. Plan your work. Come to board meetings with thick reports relating to whatever you want to discuss. "C"s are often the only ones who will read the report, but at least they'll feel you're prepared.

People Are Part Of The Process

To become more effective, "C"s must remember that conflict

is a normal part of life. Burdens can become blessings and opposition can become an opportunity to learn. They are valuable problem-solvers, but they need to improve their people skills.

Mary, the mother of Jesus, demonstrated "C" behavior when she pondered everything in her heart (Luke 2:19). This does not mean she worried a lot. It simply means she was a thinker. Mary may not have had a "C" personality, but that really doesn't matter. What matters is that God chose her for a specific reason, and she was serious about doing it right.

God uses us because of—and despite—our personalities, but He uses different people in different ways. The question for "C"s to ask themselves is, "How can God use me?" Don't worry about all your faults or all the ways God cannot use you. Concentrate and "ponder" on those things that are positive, and God will use you in a great way.

"C" parents, teachers, mates, and employees can be very difficult to live and work with. They tend to be too task-oriented, and often rub people wrong. Relationships are built on agreements, and people respond best to those who share a common bond. These naturally critical people need to learn to be more agreeable instead of judgmental. They can become very lonely people because few friends will endure their need to be right always.

"C"s often focus on correctness and miss the fellowship and feelings of others. Compromise is important to healthy relationships. Some people take offense at the thought of compromise, but it is absolutely necessary in marriage. "C" partners need to be more tolerant and forgiving. Their moodiness can kill love. Constantly pressing for perfection can discourage anyone. They need to learn to be more positive and optimistic.

Children of "C" parents often feel like they can never please their parents. The children may clean their rooms, but their rooms are never quite clean enough to suit the parent.

At work, "C" supervisors can erode good attitudes by never complementing their employees. Constant criticism (even if it is accurate) is demotivating. Try focusing on the good your employees do. It will increase their effectiveness.

"C" employees must remember to not complain too much. It makes fellow employees avoid you. It also makes management think you're not a team player, and therefore, your chances for promotions may be affected.

Conflicts

"C"s are "experts," even at conflict. They have perfected their way of finding fault in nearly everything. If there's a flaw in the plan, they will find it. They have the intuitive ability to find the weak spots, but fault-finding is extremely annoying to the dreamers and doers. "D"s inevitably clash with "C"s over implementing an idea. "D"s want to do it immediately, but "C"s want to take more time to research and prepare.

Recently I heard a story about a pastor who had a "C" elder on his board. This man was an engineer who never seemed to agree with the pastor about anything! When the pastor first came to the church, the elder who started the church (a high "D") was having difficulties with this "C" elder. The "D" elder expressed how he wished the "C" were no longer on the board, but the pastor encouraged him to be patient. The pastor was determined to patch up their differences, and one of his first duties was to visit this "C" to bridge the gap of hostility and resentment.

The two men had a wonderful visit. The elder seemed to be conscientious and caring. He and his wife had a real love for the Lord and a tremendous ministry in the church. She was head of the Women's Ministry. The pastor later discovered, however, that the Women's Ministry was a major irritation to the board, and her husband ardently defended her in board meetings.

The pastor eventually regretted his peace making tour. The "C" became the pastor's arch rival, and everything the pastor tried to do upset him. His daughter was the church pianist, and things didn't go well with her either. People complained about her—and her dad's defensiveness about her.

The pastor was in a no win position. He needed a pianist, and he wanted to minister to her because her marriage was in trouble. Also, he wanted unity on the board. The Women's Ministry had a positive impact on the church, but neither the "D" elder nor the pastor could get along with this "C."

The situation got so bad that the "C" elder once confronted the pastor about a trivial matter in his office right before the worship service. The pastor didn't want to get into it at that moment, so he proceeded toward the door explaining that they would have to talk later. He literally blocked the pastor's path. The pastor thought the elder was going to hit him! The pastor would have had to go through him to get out of his own office and go preach a sermon on God's love! He couldn't believe what was happening!

The pastor confronted the "C" elder in the next elders' meeting. The pastor was sure the "D" elder would support him, but he never said a word! The pastor was fed to the lions. Though no one ever said it, they must have concluded that the pastor was the source of the problem. Privately the elders shared the pastor's concerns about the Women's Ministry, the "C"'s defensiveness, and the poor music at church, but in the meetings, the "good ol' boy" network reigned. They all started the church together, and they were obviously committed to protecting each other.

Lack of unity cripples churches. In the past, I've had my troubles relating to church staff and boards. I've learned a lot about harmony, myself and Human Behavior Science. I can be my own worst enemy. My personality has been a source of irritation to a few people. My heart's desire is to be a lover not a fighter, but sometimes I go too far and become too soft and become a wishy washy, spineless compromiser. I need to be balanced: a man of steel and velvet at the appropriate times.

I'm responsible for *my* responses to difficult situations and difficult people. I'm not responsible for *their* responses. He is obviously breaking me. He's making me more like Jesus. God takes "D"s and "C"s to the edge and teaches them He's in control. God often uses the death of a vision, broken relationships, failed ministries, and unfulfilled expectations to teach us great lessons.

An Unforgettable Lesson

God used a dramatic situation with my son once. I thought I had to be totally in control of my children. "C" children can be finicky, and our first born was very inquisitive. His persistent questions challenged me. My typical response was, "It's not for you to question but to obey." That worked until he was almost a teenager. One day he asked why he couldn't do something. I simply said, "Because."

He thought about it for a second. Realizing that was no answer, he responded, "Why, 'because'?" Irritated, I retorted, "Because I say so."

Again he thought for a moment. He still didn't understand and questioned, "Why 'because you say so'?" Sensing defiance, I blurted, "Because I'm your father!"

He paused to think that answer over a little longer, then he concluded he still didn't understand and persisted, "Why 'because you're my father'?"

I was angry (and I didn't have the foggiest idea of a good answer), so I yelled, "Go to your room! 'Do all things without murmuring and disputing!'" But I also bit my lower lip like Ricky Ricardo on the "I Love Lucy" television show. My son began to laugh because I looked so funny.

But I didn't think it was funny in the least! I glared at him and slowly growled, "You'll never laugh at me again!" I proceeded to give him a spanking right there. I lost my cool. I never had disciplined him without first explaining why. I always made sure he understood what he had done wrong. I always did it under control . . . but not that day.

He ran to his room crying. I went to my room almost crying. I knew I had blown it. I prayed, "Lord help me understand what just happened. Help me understand myself and my son. What should I do now?"

A few months earlier, I had administered a personality profile to Curtis. I had just been certified as a "Human Behavior Consultant." When I blew up at him, I realized I needed some objectivity, so I looked at his assessment and found he is a "D/C." He is a "D" like me and a "C" like his mother, but I was treating him only like a "D."

I went to his room and said, "Son, I need to tell you something. I think I have been doing you wrong."

He said, "You're absolutely right about that, Dad!" He then said something that really hurt. He sobbed, "You've made my life so miserable for the past six months that sometimes I don't even feel like living any more." I just about died. I wanted to be the perfect father. I hardly missed any of his Little League games. I was always there for him, but something had gone wrong.

I cried, "I'm sorry, Curtis." It's hard for "D"s to say they're sorry. I then told him he could laugh at me any time I bit my lower lip. (He's laughed a few times since then.) I also promised, "I will answer your questions. I may not answer them when you ask, or I may not answer them how you want, but I promise to answer your questions."

Our relationship used to be very close. When he was a young boy, he would crawl up into my lap and whisper, "You're my Dad, and I'm your son!" In those six months, our relationship had been strained. After my humbling experience and promise to answer his questions, we began to draw close again.

Several years later, a wonderful thing happened. Curtis came home for Thanksgiving break while attending college. I was lying on the living room floor watching a football game, and he laid his head on my chest. I was so thrilled to think he felt comfortable enough to be close to me again.

I thought back when he was twelve, how I blew it and learned a tremendous lesson about loving him and answering his questions. I thought about when the apostle John lay on Jesus' breast. I thought of all the fathers who wished their teenagers wanted to be close to them. It was wonderful!

After a while, I needed to get up. I wanted to be funny, so I said, "What am I, your pillow?"

I'll never forget his answer. He simply said, "No, you're my dad." I wept quietly.

Questions, Questions, Questions

"C"s asks questions, after questions. It's not they aren't smart. In fact, "C"s tend to be very inquisitive and great learners. They need to guard their constant search for answers and learn how to be happy without understanding everything.

"C"s make great students, if their teachers satisfy their quest for knowledge and understanding. "C"s need to avoid against becoming moody, if their search is not being satisfied. The Bible teaches us to be content, no matter what state we're in.

"C"s make the most competent, yet often most challenging to work and live with.

11

Discovering Your Behavioral Blends

I believe God places the unmistakable quality of life and personality within each of us at conception, and He fashions us in the womb (Job 31:15). Our pre-birth personality development has already begun to take form even before our first breath. Our parents, environment, and early childhood experiences continue to shape our unique personalities, and we become the products of many influences which touch our young lives.

Our personalities are composites of four identifiable temperaments. No blend is better than the other. Each blend simply describes the complexity of our personalities. Only 15% of people have a predominate "D" or "I" or "S" or "C" personality. The other 85% have a mixture of two or three specific types such as:
•"D/I" •"S/C" •"I/S" •"D/C" •"I/C" •"D/S," or •"I/S/C"

There are actually 256 possible composites, but we will focus on twenty-one behavioral blends. 1 Corinthians 15:39-41 emphasizes the diversity in nature. There are many different kinds of animals, stars, and people. There are 150 or so different kinds of dogs, but they are all canines. Each breed of dog is different, yet they are similar in many ways. In the same way, there are many different kinds of behavior, but they are all part of the complexity of human personalities.

Pressure and stress reveal what we're made of: our temperaments as well as our character. Adversity has a way of demonstrating and refining our personalities. Just as fire and heat temper steel, our problems can strengthen us. Our personalities are influenced by both our flesh and the Holy Spirit within us. How we respond will determine how God blesses or disciplines us. Each behavioral blend has its unique ways of responding or reacting to pressure. Spiritual growth occurs when we allow the Holy Spirit to control us.

Adversity is like the clay in the potter's hand. The potter carefully applies pressure to mold the clay into a vessel. In the same way, God uses stress and problems to conform us into the image of Christ.

Behavioral Blends

Study the brief paragraph descriptions in this section. You may be a combination of two specific profiles. You can also have some characteristics of other types, but usually, people fit into one or two behavioral blends. Each set of descriptions begins with a brief summary of the single, unblended personality type which is followed by blends of that type.

Dr. John Geier, who developed the original Performax Personal Profile System, originally identified 18 blends which he called "Classical Patterns." His research concluded that these patterns were the most common blends. Since that time, Dr. Geier has added three more patterns which are blends of three types. Please note: There are two "D/I"s but no "D/S." The two are included because there are two distinct varieties of this blend, and the "D/S" is omitted because these people are described in the "S/D" blend.

D: "Determined Doers"

"D"s are dominant and demanding, and they want to win at all costs. They don't care about what people think; they want to get the job done! They are insensitive to others' feelings. They are determined to get going, but they need to be more attentive to details. They are motivated by serious challenges to accomplish tasks.

D/I: "Driving Influencers"

"D/I"s are bottom line people. They are much like Dynamic Influencers (see next paragraph), but Driving Influencers are more determined and less inspirational. They are strong doers and able to encourage others to follow. They need to be more cautious and steady. They often get involved in too many projects, so they need to slow down and focus on one thing at a time. They are motivated by opportunities to accomplish great tasks through a lot of people.

D/I: "Dynamic Influencers"

"D/I"s are impressive and demanding. They get excited about accomplishing tasks and looking good. Determined and driven, they influence large crowds best. They can be too strong and too concerned about what others think. They have good communication skills and are interested in people, but they need to be more sensitive and patient with the feelings of others. Slowing down and thinking through projects are crucial. They are motivated by opportunities to control and impress.

D/C: "Driven and Competent"

"D/C"s are determined students or defiant critics. They want to be in charge while they collect information to accomplish tasks. They care more about getting a job done and doing it right than what others think or feel. They drive themselves and others, and they are dominant and caustic. Improving their people skills is important, and they need to be more sensitive and understanding. They are motivated by choices and challenges to do well.

I: "Inspirational Influencers"

"I"s are impressive people. They are active and excited individuals. Approval is important to them. They can have lots of friends if they don't overwhelm people with their enthusiasm. They can be sensitive and emotional, but they need to be more interested in others and willing to listen. They don't like research unless it makes them look good. They often do things to please the crowd because they are entertainers. They need to control their feelings and think more logically. They often outshine others and are motivated by recognition.

I/D: "Inspirational Doers"

"I/D"s are super salespeople. They love large groups. They are impressive and can easily influence people. They need a lot of recognition, and they often exaggerate and talk too much. They jump into things without thinking them through, so they need to be more studious, reflective, and cautious. They are motivated by exciting opportunities to do difficult things. If they aren't careful, they live to please the crowd and get themselves into trouble. They make inspiring and determined leaders.

I/S: "Inspirational Specialists"

"I/S"s are influential and stable. They love people and people love them. They like to please and serve others, but they don't like time controls or difficult tasks. They want to look good and encourage others, but they often lack organizational skills. They follow directions and do what they are told, but they should be more concerned about what to do, than with whom to do it. They are motivated by interaction and sincere opportunities to help others. Whether they are up front or behind the scenes, they like to influence and support others. They make good friends and obedient workers.

I/C: "Inspirational and Competent"

"I/C"s are inspiring yet cautious. They size up situations and comply with the rules in order to look good. They are adept at figuring out ways to do things better through a lot of people, but they can be too persuasive and too concerned about winning. They are often impatient and critical, and they need to be more sensitive to individual feelings even though they are very sensitive about what others think of them. They don't like breaking the rules, and they don't enjoy taking risks. They need to try new things and sometimes go against the crowd. They are careful communicators.

S: "Steady Specialists"

"S"s are stable and shy, and they don't like changes. They enjoy pleasing people and can perform repetitive tasks. Secure, non-threatening surroundings are important to them. They make good friends because they are so forgiving, but other people sometimes take advantage of them. They need to be stronger and learn how to say "No." Talking in front of large crowds is usually difficult for them. They are motivated by opportunities to help others.

S/I: "Steady Influencers"

"S/I"s are sensitive and inspirational. They have lots of friends because they are tolerant and forgiving. They don't hurt people's feelings and can be very influential, but they need to be more task-oriented. They need to learn to finish their work and do it well. They like to talk and should pay more attention to instructions. They are kind and considerate, but they would be more influential if they were more aggressive and careful. Motivated by opportunities to share and shine, they readily induce others to follow them.

S/D: "Steady Doers"

"S/D"s get the job done. They prefer stable surroundings and are determined to accomplish tasks. As quiet leaders, they relate best to small groups. They don't like to talk in front of large crowds, but they want to control them. They enjoy secure relationships, but too often try to dominate people. They are motivated by sincere challenges that allow them to accomplish tasks systematically. They make good friends even though they have a driving desire to succeed.

S/C: "Steady and Competent"

"S/C"s are stable and contemplative people. They like to research and discover the facts, and they like to weigh the evidence and proceed slowly to a logical conclusion. They enjoy small groups of people, but they don't like speaking in front of large crowds. They are systematic and sensitive to the needs of others, but they can also be critical and caustic. They are loyal friends but can be too fault-finding. They need to work on their enthusiasm and optimism. They are motivated by kindness and by opportunities to accomplish tasks slowly and correctly.

C: "Cautious Competent"

"C"s are logical and analytical. Their predominant drive is careful, calculating, compliant, and correct behavior. When they feel frustrated, they may withdraw in despair, or in contrast, they may become hyperactive. They need others to answer their questions patiently. They aren't sensitive to the feelings of others, and they can be critical and crabby. They prefer quality and reject phoniness in others. They are motivated by explanations and projects that stimulate their thinking.

C/S: "Competent Specialists"

"C/S"s have to be right. They like to do one thing at a time and do it right the first time. Their steady and stable approach to things makes them reserved and cautious. They are consistent and careful, but seldom take risks or try new things. They don't like speaking to large crowds but will work hard behind the scenes to help groups stay on track. They are motivated by opportunities to serve others and to do things correctly.

C/I/S: "Competent, Influencing Specialists"

"C/I/S"s like to do things right, impress others, and stabilize situations. They aren't aggressive or pushy people. They enjoy both large and small crowds. They are good with people and do quality work. They are sensitive to what others think about them and their work. They need to be more determined and dominant. They can do things well, but are slow in decision-making. They are capable of doing great things through people, but they need to be more self-motivated and assertive. They are stimulated by sincere, enthusiastic approval and logical explanations.

C/S/D: "Competent, Steady Doers"

"C/S/D"s are a combination of cautious, stable, and determined types of people. They are task-oriented, but they care about people on an individual basis. They don't like to speak in front of crowds. They prefer to get the job done—and do it right—through small groups instead of large groups. They tend to be serious and are often misunderstood by others as being insensitive. "C/S/D" types really care for people, but they just don't show it openly. They need to be more positive and enthusiastic. Natural achievers, they need to be more friendly and less critical.

I/D/S: "Inspiring, Driving, and Submissive"

"I/D/S"s are impressive, demanding, and stable. They are not as cautious and calculating as those with greater "C" tendencies. They are fairly active, but they are sensitive and steady. They seem to be people-oriented, but they can be dominant and decisive in their task-orientation. They need to be more contemplative and conservative. Taking charge and working with people are more important to them than details.

D/I/C: "Dominant, Inspiring, and Cautious"

"D/I/C"s are demanding, impressive, and competent. They tend to be task-oriented, but they are comfortable before crowds. They need to increase their sensitivity to others. They don't mind change. Active and outgoing, they are also compliant and cautious. They like to do things correctly, but they also influence others to follow because their verbal skills combine with their determination and competence. Security is not as important to them as looking good.

Straight Mid-Line

A Straight Mid-Line Blend occurs when all four plotting points on the DISC assessment are in the middle area of the graph. This may indicate that the person is trying to please everyone. Striving to be "all things to all men" may be a mature response to pressure, or it may show that the person is experiencing intense frustration. When this person takes the profile, he may answer in ways he thinks others want him to answer instead of his real thoughts and preferences. He can complete another profile several months later to get a more accurate reading.

Above Mid-Line

Some patterns indicate unique struggles an individual may be having. An Above Mid-Line Blend occurs when all four plotting points are above the mid-line. This may indicate the person feels compelled to over-achieve.

Below Mid-Line

A Below Mid-Line Blend occurs when all four plotting points are below the mid-line. This may indicate that the person feels insecure and is not really sure how to respond to challenges.

Biblical Applications

When we discover our personalities, we can recognize areas God wants to work on. The Bible is our best source of help. "All Scripture is given by inspiration of God and is profitable for doctrine, for reproof, correction, for instruction in righteousness," 2 Timothy 3:16. The following passages of Scripture are admonitions and challenges to help you focus on becoming more like Christ. These passages apply to all of us, but they are especially pertinent in our areas of weakness and need.

D: "Determined Doers"

- Be careful to not offend people when you take charge. "The servant of the Lord must not strive (be pushy), but be gentle" (2 Tim. 2:24).
- Anger is a normal human emotion, but it must be controlled. "Be angry and sin not" (Eph. 4:26).
- Pursue purity and peace. "Wisdom from above is first pure, peaceable . . ." (James 3:17).
- Focus on doing one thing well. "This one thing I do" (Phil. 3:13).
- Always remember, God is the Master of your fate. "The fear of

the Lord is the beginning of wisdom" (Prov. 1:7).

D/I: "Driving Influencers"

- Though naturally fearless and able, you need to respect God's power over you. "Fear God and give Him glory" (Rev. 14:7).
- Guard the overuse of strength; be kind. "By the meekness and gentleness of Christ" (2 Cor. 10:1).
- Making peace is a greater challenge than winning a fight. "Blessed are the peacemakers" (Matt. 5:9).
- Choose your words carefully. "A soft answer turns away wrath" (Prov. 15:1).
- Let God control your feelings. "The fruit of the Spirit is . . . temperance (self-control)" (Gal. 5:23).

D/I: "Dynamic Influencers"

- Develop humility and obedience. Christ "humbled Himself and became obedient" (Phil. 2:8).
- Everyone has a boss, even you. "I too am a man under authority" (Matt. 8:9).
- Avoid rebellion. "Rebellion is as the sin of witchcraft" (1 Sam. 15:23).
- Winning is not always most important. "The first shall be last" (Matt. 19:30).
- Be patient with others. "The fruit of the Spirit is long-suffering" (Gal. 5:23).
- Learn to trust in the Lord instead of your ability to make things happen. "Rest in the Lord" (Psa. 37:7).

D/C: "Driven and Competent"

- Seek to get along with everyone. "Live peaceable with all men" (Rom. 12:18).
- Be kind and loving. "Kindly affectionate one to another" (Rom.

12:10).
- Show more love. "Love one another" (1 John 4:7).
- Seek to serve, not to be served. Be a "servant of Christ" (Eph. 6:6).
- Meekness is not weakness. Control your desire for power over others. "By the meekness and gentleness of Christ" (2 Cor. 10:1).
- Take time to be still and commune with God. "Be still and know that I am God" (Psa. 46:10).

I: "Inspirational Influencers"
- Don't exalt yourself. "Humble yourself and God will exalt you" (James 4:10).
- Listen more. "Be quick to hear, slow to speak" (James 1:19).
- Work at being organized. "Do all things decently and in order" (1 Cor. 14:40).
- Concentrate on doing what is most important. "All things are not expedient" (1 Cor. 10:23).
- Prepare thoroughly. "Prepare yourself" (2 Chron. 35:4).
- Be careful what you desire. "Delight in the Lord" (Prov. 3:5,6).
- Don't be overconfident; watch what you promise. Peter claimed he would never deny Christ (Mark 14:31).
- You are to be the reflection of Christ (Rom. 8:29).

I/D: "Inspirational Doers"
- Guard the power of your words. "The tongue is a fire" (James 3:6).
- Don't be like those who "by fair words and good speeches deceive" (Rom. 16:18).
- Always tell the truth. "Speak the truth and lie not" (1 Tim. 2:7).
- Remember who has blessed you. "God must increase, I must

decrease" (John 3:30).
- Give God the glory for all you do. "Give unto the Lord glory" (Psa. 29:1,2).
- Put God first in your life. "Seek you first the kingdom of God" (Matt. 6:33).
- Beware of the "lust of the flesh and pride of life" because they will ultimately destroy your talents (1 John 2:16).

I/S: "Inspirational Specialists"
- Do everything unto the Lord. "Whatsoever you do, do it heartedly as unto the Lord and not unto men" (Col. 3:23).
- Beware of seeking man's approval. "Not with eyeservice as men pleasers" (Eph. 6:6).
- Seek to please God rather than others. "Do always those things that please Him" (John 8:29).
- Be more task-oriented. "Sit down first and count the cost" (Luke 14:28).
- Don't be lazy. "Not slothful in business" (Rom. 12:11).
- Work hard. "Let every man prove his work" (Gal. 6:4).
- Don't just talk about what you want. "Being fruitful in every good work" (Col. 1:10).
- Be industrious. "Night comes when no man can work" (John 9:4).

I/C: "Inspirational and Competent"
- Don't think too highly of yourself. "God resists the proud but gives grace to the humble" (1 Pet. 5:5).
- Seek to please God more than others. "When a man's ways please the Lord" (Prov. 16:7).
- Be a good example. "Be an example of the believer" (1 Tim. 4:12).
- Care more about how you look to God. "Glorify God in your

body" (1 Cor. 6:20).
- Be bold and confident in Christ. "We have boldness and access with confidence by the faith of Him" (Eph. 3:12).
- Guard what you say. "A lying tongue is a vanity tossed to and fro" (Prov. 21:6).
- Don't flatter yourself. "He flatters himself in his own eyes" (Psa. 36:2).

S: "Steady Specialists"
- Increase your confidence in Christ. "I can do all things through Christ who strengthens me" (Phil. 4:13).
- God is your "rock, fortress, and deliverer" (Psa. 18:2).
- Fear is not from God. "God has not given you the spirit of fear" (2 Tim. 1:7).
- Speak out more often. "Let the redeemed of the Lord say so" (Psa. 107:2).
- Be outgoing and less inhibited. "Christ has made us free" (Gal. 5:1).
- Be assertive. Moses confronted Pharaoh, "Let my people go!" (Ex. 5:1).
- Security is possible. "You are secure because of hope" (Job 11:18).

S/I: "Steady Influencers"
- Speak out. "Bold to speak without fear" (Phil. 1:14).
- Take stands. "Steadfast in one spirit" (Phil. 4:1).
- The Spirit of God can help you tell others about Christ. "The Spirit of the Lord is upon me" (Isa. 61:1).
- Guard against fearfulness. "Let not your heart be troubled, neither let it be afraid" (Luke 14:27).
- Remember, you don't always need people to encourage you. "David encouraged himself in the Lord" (1 Sam. 30:6).

- Always do right and don't fear people. "Fear of man brings a snare (trap)" (Psa. 29:25).

S/D: "Steady Doers"

- God wants to empower you. "Most gladly will I rather glory in my infirmities that the power of Christ may rest upon me."
- God's grace (the power and ability to do what God wants) is enough for whatever you need. "My grace is sufficient for you."
- You are strong in weakness as you trust in God. "For when I am weak, then am I strong" (2 Cor. 12:9).
- Encourage and help others daily. "Exhort one another daily" (Heb. 3:13).
- God invites you to reason with Him. "Come now and let us reason together" (Isa. 1:18).

S/C: "Steady and Competent"

- Be assertive and strong. "Only be strong and very courageous" (Joshua 1:6).
- Be more enthusiastic. "Whatever you do, do it heartedly" (Col. 3:23).
- Enjoy relationships rather than endure them. Christ said, "I am come that you might have life and have it abundantly" (John 10:10).
- Peace and happiness do not come from security and safety. "Peace I leave with you, my peace I give unto you" (John 14:27).
- Divine peace is knowing God's ways are beyond ours. "The peace of God passes all understanding" (Phil. 4:7).
- Be fearless in Christ. "I will fear no evil" (Psa. 23:4).

C: "Cautious and Competent"

- Be more patient when you correct others. "Rebuke, exhort

with all long suffering" (2 Tim. 4:2).
- Correct others in love. "Speak the truth in love" (Eph. 4:15).
- Be more positive. "Rejoice in the Lord always" (Phil. 4:4).
- Hope in God, not your circumstances. "Rejoicing in hope" (Rom. 12:12).
- The most logical thing you can do is serve God. "Present your body a living sacrifice . . . which is your reasonable service" (Rom 12:2).
- Find happiness in God. "Delight in the Lord" (Psa. 37:4).

C/S: "Competent Specialists"
- Think more positively. "Whatsoever things are pure . . . of good report . . . think on those things" (Phil. 4:8,9).
- Guard against the fear of failure. God commands: "Fear not for I am with you" (Isa. 43:5).
- Focus on the possible. "With God all things are possible" (Matt. 19:26).
- Be cheerful. "The fruit of the Spirit is . . . joy" (Gal. 5:22).
- When everything goes wrong, God is all you need. "Our sufficiency is of God" (2 Cor. 3:5).
- Have the mind of Christ. "Let this mind be in you that was also in Christ" (Phil. 4:8).

C/I/S: "Competent, Influencing Specialists"
- Guard against being judgmental. "Judge not lest you be judged" (Matt. 7:1). "Who are you that judges another," James 4:12.
- Avoid bitterness and resentment. "Lest any root of bitterness spring up to trouble you" (Heb. 12:15).
- God will meet your needs. "My God shall supply all your need according to His riches in glory" (Phil. 4:19).
- Be thankful for everything. "In all things give thanks" (1

Thess. 5:18).

- Let God's Word encourage and guide you. "Let the Word of God dwell in you richly in all wisdom" (Col. 3:16).
- Whatever you do, do it for God's glory. "Do all in the name of God" (Col. 3:17).

C/S/D: "Competent, Steady Doers"

- Be more enthusiastic. "Whatever you do, do it heartedly as unto the Lord" (Col. 3:23).
- Don't worry so much about problems. "Let not your heart be troubled" (John 14:27).
- Be more positive. "Whatsoever things are pure . . . if there be any virtue, think on these things" (Phil. 4:8,9).
- Be more sensitive. "Be kindly affectionate, one to another" (Rom. 12:10).
- Don't be like Moses when he was reluctant to lead because of his poor verbal skills (Ex. 4:10-16).
- Be more outwardly optimistic and encouraging to others. "Exhort one another daily" (Heb. 3:13).

I/D/S: "Inspiring, Driving, and Submissive"

- Be more calculating and careful. "Sit down first and count the cost" (Luke 14:28).
- Be more organized. "Do all things decently and in order" (1 Cor. 14:40).
- Be careful what you promise. "Let you 'yea' be 'yea' and your 'nay' be 'nay'" (2 Cor. 1:17).
- Give God the glory for all you do. "Give unto the Lord glory" (Psa. 29:1,2).
- Think before you act. "Plans fail for lack of counsel" (Prov. 15:22).
- Be humble and share the glory. "Humble yourself and God will

exalt you" (James 4:10).

D/I/C: "Dominant, Inspiring, and Cautious"

- Listen more. "Quick to hear, slow to speak" (James 1:19).
- Be more sensitive to other's feelings. "The servant of the Lord must not strive, but be gentle" (2 Tim. 2:24).
- Be a peacemaker. "Blessed are the peacemakers" (Matt. 5:9).
- Be steady; don't get sidetracked. "Be steadfast always doing the work of the Lord" (1 Cor. 15:58).
- Don't be judgmental. "If a man be overtaken in a fault, restore him" (Gal. 6:1).
- Be optimistic and encouraging to others. "Exhort one another daily" (Heb. 3:13).

Straight Mid-Line

- Recognize your identity in Christ. "I am crucified with Christ, nevertheless I live, yet not I, but Christ lives in me" (Gal. 2:20).
- Relax in the Lord. "Come unto me all you that labor and are heavy laden, and I will give you rest" (Matt. 11:28).
- You cannot please everyone all the time. "Be imitators of God as dearly beloved children" (Eph. 5:1).

Above Mid-Line

- An Above Mid-Line Blend may be trying of over-achieve. "It is God who works in us, both to will and do of His good pleasure" (Phil. 2:13).
- You may feel pressure from unrealistic expectations. Remember Peter.

Below Mid-Line

- A Below Mid-Line Blend may indicate you feel threatened by

challenges. "I can do all things through Christ" (Phil. 4:13).
• Think more positively about yourself. "I am fearfully and
  wonderfully made" (Psa. 139:14).

You may benefit from memorizing one or more of these passages which are particularly meaningful to you. As you "hide God's Word in your heart," you can draw on its wisdom and strength more readily. You can begin by choosing one passage and writing it on a card. Put the card in your pocket so you can pull it out and read it several times a day. Soon, you will know the verse by heart! As you memorize it, reflect on each word. This exercise will enable you to apply it more specifically in your circumstances and relationships.

12

Choices and Changes: Practical Applications

Each of us needs specific, practical applications to enhance our strengths and avoid our weaknesses. This chapter contains general suggestions to help people of each personality type.

Seeing our behavior in others can help us understand ourselves. By recognizing the "quirks" of those around us, we can improve our own behavior. Often, the things we hate in others are the very things we struggle with in our own lives. Scripture applies this principle to marriage in 1 Peter 3:7. It teaches us to "Dwell with 'our wives' according to knowledge." How do we do this?

I dwell with my Honda according to knowledge because I know when to change the oil, rotate the tires, and give the car a tune up. I know how to make my Honda operate at maximum efficiency.

When I married, I knew very little about my wife. In fact, I knew very little about dwelling with anyone according to knowledge. I didn't know why others did what they did—what made them tick. I had a lot to learn about living and working with people. I became a student of my wife, her needs, her moods, her desires, and her behavior. Everyday I learn more and that knowledge helps me respond more appropriately to her.

Wisdom That Works

Practical application is making knowledge work. If we don't know how to use knowledge, it's worthless. Being people smart is knowing why people do what they do, but being personality wise is knowing what to do about it. The tragedy in most relationships is that people don't even have the basic knowledge of human behavior. Understanding how and why we are the way we are is important, but practical application is what makes our knowledge powerful. After all is said and done, we need to apply what we learn. The goal is to apply truth in our specific areas of improvement. Life is a journey toward maturity. We're always improving but never arriving. It's a challenge and an adventure, a steady and reasonable journey.

Did you notice that I used D, I, S, and C terms in the last sentence? "D"s respond to challenges. "I"s love the adventure. "S"s desire steady and stable emphasis, and "C"s look for the reasonable things. We respond to life according to our personalities.

Practical application helps us recognize our strengths and weaknesses so that we use our strengths wisely and overcome our weaknesses. Some of the greatest lessons come from on-the-job training. All the books and seminars in the world can never compare to the lessons we learn from life's experiences.

Experience is a great teacher. The problem is we often fail to learn from our experiences. Someone has said, "The only thing we learn from history is that we don't learn from history." We have learned that people respond in many different ways. We respond according to our own personalities, but each person we meet with has his or her own personality, and the clash of different temperaments causes conflict.

Volumes have been written about human behavior, but wis-

20

dom is attained only by using the knowledge we acquire. Learning provides knowledge, but wisdom provides practical application.

Practical Application for "D"s

"D"s must learn how to be team players. Their desire to be in charge tempts them to fly solo. Although they may be able to do some things better by themselves, they can be more influential as part of a team. Philippians 1:27 challenges us to strive together for the faith, but working with others can be difficult for these driven people because they like to take control and push forward. They need to train themselves to include others in their decision-making. They also need to be aware of the needs and drives of others.

Working with "D"s who refuse to play second fiddle to anyone can be exasperating. Often they don't understand their emotions and actions. They can benefit from a clear explanation of why they have such determination.

Choices, Not Commands

"D"s don't like being told what to do, so it is important to give them choices. Instead of telling a "D" child that he must go to bed at 9:00, tell him he can choose between going to bed at 8:30 or 9:00. Ask him, "Which time do you choose?"

Explain who's the boss, and teach them responsibility by allowing them to make some decisions for themselves. Make sure they realize that there are consequences if they do not act responsibly. Get "D" children to agree beforehand on the punishment or discipline they will receive if they violate the rules.

Joshua challenged the children of Israel: "Choose you this day whom you will serve" (Joshua 24:15). "D"s love straightforward confrontation. "D"s who are Christian leaders challenge everyone to get right with God. Under the filling power of the Spirit, these dominant leaders are very effective, but in the flesh, they can be disastrous.

Don't let "D"s control you. They need parameters for their behavior and actions. They stretch the limits, so you must let them know how far is too far. They desperately need good role models for self-control. Show them how to stay in control by remaining calm while dealing with them.

Meekness Is Not Weakness

"D"s should be taught that meekness is not weakness. Jesus, the most powerful man who ever lived, was meek. Meekness is power under control. The harder it is to stay in control, the more important meekness will be. During the early part of his ministry, Jesus startled the crowd with the Sermon on the Mount statement, "Blessed are the meek" (Matthew 5:5). The Roman world believed that meekness was a weakness. Seneca, a Roman philosopher, wrote that meekness was "the disease of the soul." With the backdrop of this thinking, Jesus dropped the bomb of validating meekness.

Jesus taught that God was giving them a new way of thinking and believing. He wanted to give them freedom from themselves. Anyone can argue about anger, but the meek can control their anger. Anyone can blow his or her top, but those who are truly meek are able to control their feelings and actions. "D"s who struggle with anger should literally walk away from an explosive situation. They should not do what comes naturally—what they feel like doing at the moment. Chances are, that is the worst thing they could do! Paul wrote, "The servant of the Lord must not strive, but be gentle" (2 Timothy 2:5). The word "strive" means "to war, to quarrel, to fight." Christians should be the strongest but most gentle people on earth.

Driven, determined people are most effective and influential when they are not threatened. Don't push them! They tend to respond like wild animals that have been cornered. They attack! Give them a way out by giving them a choice or negotiating a settlement in which they are able to save face and not feel intimidated.

"D"s Under Authority

"D"s must learn to respect authority figures such as the police, teachers, and bosses, even though these people seem to make life difficult. They don't enjoy being submissive. There's something in them that cries for independence and wants freedom, but the worst bondage is enslavement to one's own emotions and actions. True freedom comes through being under authority.

We cannot truly possess authority until we learn to submit to authority. The most powerful people in the world are under some type of authority. When they learn to work in healthy dependence on others instead of defiant independence, they will be more successful. Jesus never did anything apart from His Father's permission. Jesus often demonstrated a "not my will, but they will be done" attitude.

"D"s typically see submission as weak or cowardly, but this can be used as a tremendous opportunity to show them what strength under control really means. They lose their authority if they lose the respect of others. Then they have no platform to influence people. Understanding the principle of respect for authority is imperative for them. When Jesus completed His Sermon on the Mount, the people said, "He taught as one having authority" (Matthew 7:29). Jesus began His message talking about meekness and ended His message with tremendous demonstration of the power of God in His life.

Showing Feelings

"D"s also need to learn how to show their emotions without

blowing their tops. Their short fuses get them into trouble. When faced with opposition, people must choose between reacting and responding. There's a big difference! Responding is measured and controlled; it is based on wisdom. Reacting is saying whatever comes off the top of your head in spite of its affects on others. Reacting is lighting dynamite; responding defuses it. When you respond rather than react, you remain in control. Learning to respond properly is perhaps their greatest challenge.

Showing feelings of warmth and kindness is difficult for demanding, dominant people. They see crying as a sign of weakness. Expressing your feelings is allowing yourself to be transparent with others. Even Jesus wept (Matthew 11:35).

Crushed Through Crisis

Most "D"s haven't ever been broken. They're so full of themselves that they can lose their effectiveness in helping others. They want to control everyone and everything but haven't learned to control themselves. (I know. I've learned this through my own experiences.) God dealt with these types of people in the Scriptures in ways that got their attention. Paul was blinded on the Damascus Road. Jacob had to wrestle with the Lord all night.

Crises teach them to be humble. Once they realize they aren't as infallible and powerful as they thought, "D"s become broken. Out of that brokenness comes a more sensitive attitude toward others. One of my few original sayings is, "Let crisis draw you closer to where Christ is." Like a storm, there is an eye in every crisis. Christ is in the center of every turbulence, ready to calm and control us. He has greater victories in store than we could ever experience apart from the storm.

When Jesus told the disciples, "Take my yoke upon you and learn of me. For my yoke is easy and my burden is light" (Matthew 11:29-30), they must have thought Jesus was absolutely crazy! John the Baptist was in jail. The disciples had no place to sleep, no money, and few followers. Jesus, however, was comparing His burdens with theirs. His yoke and burden are easier than carrying theirs alone. Going through the trials of life with this perspective makes the storms easier to bear. Crisis has a way of bringing even the toughest people down to size. "D"s can turn a crisis into a challenge by controlling themselves.

Practical Application for "I"s

"I"s are driven by their strong desire to impress and influence others. They want to be recognized for their accomplishments, because rewards are important to them. Speak positively about them in public. Parents would be wise to phone a friend or relative and share how pleased they are about their child's accomplishments. Every child deserves this, but these children thrive on personal recognition.

"I"s like to look good. I remember once opening the back door of our home and shouting to the entire neighborhood, "I want everyone to know how proud I am of my son." He just stood there with a big grin on his face. Another time, I pretended to call the President of the United States and tell him how wonderful my son was. He knew I was only pretending, but he still loved my show of attention.

The "I"s Have It

"I"s enjoy excitement—the more enthusiasm, the better! Some parents may really have to work hard to get excited, but it pays off for an "I" child. Colossians 3:23 encourages us, "Whatsoever you do, do it heartily." That means to do things with enthusiasm. "I"s love this verse, but those working with them often think they overdo it. "I"s long for group activities. They don't like to play alone; they need frequent interaction with others.

Some parents can't take much noise, so they avoid having their children's friends in their homes for any length of time. Parents of "I" children should work with their child's individual need for group interaction. Find ways the children can play without so much noise and confusion. Try letting them watch an exciting video program for children, or encourage them to do a play. Pretend that you are a movie agent and you heard how talented the group is. Ask them to write, direct, and act out their own show for you. That ought to keep them busy for a while! This will also give your "I" child the opportunity to inspire and impress.

Understand that these children may get overly excited. They tend to be too enthusiastic, which makes their parents avoid group activities. But remember, these children need more socialization than others, and it will benefit them to be involved in group activities.

Group Activities

Consider enrolling your "I" child in group activities with a trained teacher or instructor because a structured environment is better for both the parent and the child. Don't just drop off and pick up your child. Bring your camera or camcorder and take lots of pictures. Your child will love it!

Church is an excellent place for "I"s to find friendships. The Bible tells every believer not to "forsake the assembling together of the saints" (Hebrews 10:25). Regular fellowship and worship can be stimulating to them. The challenge is finding a church with consistently exciting programs and enthusiastic atmospheres that meet their interests.

"I"s need opportunities to express themselves. Asking them to obey without allowing them to question or share their feelings can be frustrating for them. It's not that they are questioning authority; they simply need to talk when they feel pressure. Given enough time, some "I"s will even talk themselves into doing what they resisted. Don't try to "out talk" them. Wait patiently and listen until they are ready for your response. That may never happen, so ask them to let you talk when they are finished. They will probably interrupt you and take off on another long-winded discourse. Again, wait for a while and then remind them you never finished. This may happen several times, but each time you are building a stronger case for them to learn they need to improve their listening skills.

They Talk Too Much

Once they realize how patient you have been (and how rude they have been!), you will have enough time to share your thoughts. They probably won't listen well, but it will make them think. This process helps "I"s to understand what you are trying to say.

It's usually a good idea to ask "I"s to share what they think you have just said to them. Don't condemn them for not listening if they get it wrong. Simply question yourself for possibly not making your words clear enough, and then rephrase your statement. Give them another chance to explain what you are saying until you both come to an agreement about the conversation. "I"s are good talkers but poor listeners. Scripture teaches, "Let every man be quick to hear, slow to speak, slow to wrath" (James 1:19). That is great advice for everyone, but "I"s especially need to learn how to be slow to speak and quick to hear.

"I"s need to learn how to share the limelight. They are usually talented, and they love to show off, but they may have a problem with pride and an intense desire for others to notice them. Help them overcome this tendency by complimenting their ability to handle losing or by explaining how impressed you are when they are willing to play second fiddle. It takes a big person to allow others to receive the credit he may deserve.

It would be good for them to remember that God will not share His glory with another (Isaiah 42:8). They often forget their responsibility to give God all the glory for successes in their lives. Isaiah 42:12 tells us to "give glory to God." Isaiah 43:7 explains He has created man for His glory. Revelation 4:11 reads, "For thy pleasure they are and were created." We were designed to bring glory and pleasure to God. When Jesus was baptized in the River Jordan, the voice from heaven said, "This is my beloved Son in whom I am well pleased" (Matthew 3:17). Jesus' only ambition in life was to please His father.

"I"s would be wise to remember who they serve. They are often enamored by their own talents and abilities, and they love to be praised by others. God may use a less talented person who is willing to give God all the credit rather than a more talented individual who is seeking his own honor. God uses people of great availability more than people of great ability. Their desire for notoriety and significance affects their feelings and actions. Their drive to inspire and influence others is often motivated by a desire to feel important. This motivation gets them into a lot of trouble! They need to evaluate why they do what they do, then choose to honor the Lord.

Disciplined Feelings

"I"s need to learn how to reflect and study. Those who are students have the potential to make excellent grades, but they sometimes fail because they socialize too much. They don't like to miss any of the action anywhere! Parents can use the "I" child's desire to impress others as a means of encouraging him to obtain better grades. Reward them with the kind of things that will improve their self-images, like new clothing or a phone of their own. Also, use discipline which motivates them to study, such as no phone privileges until they have finished their studies.

Suggest that they study with a friend, preferably a "C," who will help the "I" be more thorough in his work. Use video or cassette resources to help maintain his attention span. Find creative teaching methods to relieve them from sitting still for long periods. Get them to study in shorter intervals, ten or fifteen minutes at a time, and encourage them to tell you what they have learned. Invite them to communicate it in a song or even a rap. This may test your patience as a parent, but it could be exactly the motivation the child needs to succeed.

Scripture tells us to "be still and know that I am God" (Psalm 46:10), but these enthusiastic, energetic people don't like to sit still. They are active, people-oriented and love to impress others. They need to remember that the most important One to impress is God.

"I"s have the ability to outshine most others. They are naturally the center of attention. The problem comes when they live primarily to get that attention. God is a jealous God. He alone is worthy of praise and honor. He alone has the right to be jealous because He is the only One Who deserves all the glory. When believers desire for God to glorify God, then God honors them.

Practical Application for "S"s

"S"s respond best to kind, thoughtful people. Avoid raising your voice or losing your temper with them. They need to be in secure, calm environments to function at their best. Scripture teaches, "A soft answer turns away wrath" (Proverbs 15:1). That is applicable for everyone, but especially for these sensitive people. They don't respond well to intense or loud behavior. They back away from unstable situations and unsettling challenges. They aren't risk-takers and aren't comfortable around aggressive people. If possible, avoid putting them on the spot.

"S"s don't become easily excited. They may sometimes seem

to be disinterested or bored, but it is simply their steady nature to appear so. They are likely to become your best friends because of their sense of undying loyalty. They will stand by you and help you in any way they can.

Jesus demonstrated the greatest strength of an "S," being a friend who sticks closer than a brother (Proverbs 18:24). A true friend loves at all times (Proverbs 17:17), and "S"s seem to have this characteristic more than other personality types.

Time To Recover

Give "S"s plenty of time to adjust. They prefer slow and gradual changes and need time to respond without being pushed. They don't like surprises. If you know there is going to be a change, warn them far enough in advance so they can prepare for it. They usually aren't resistant people, but they will be less than enthusiastic if they aren't given enough space and time to adapt to change.

High touch is important to them, and they want to feel like a part of the family. Greet them by hugging or grasping their hand with both of yours. Everyone needs intimacy, but "S"s respond the best to a warm and sincere touch.

People-oriented individuals must learn to guard against being naive. They tend to be manipulated by others because of their kind and gentle demeanor, and one of the most important things "S"s need to learn is how to say "No." They tend agree to do everything people ask them to do. They are vulnerable; people take advantage of them.

Assertiveness training is a practical help. As difficult as they may find it, they can learn to stand strong. Their love for people and sense of loyalty make them easy prey for opportunistic, unscrupulous individuals. They need to be cautious and ask questions before they trust others. "S"s shouldn't feel guilty for saying "No" or worry that they may have hurt people or let the group down.

Someone else can do the task they declined.

Don't Work Harder. Think Smarter.

"S"s need to learn how to turn a request for help into an opportunity to challenge others. They can be more assertive and stimulate others to take more responsibility. They can be bold enough to challenge a "D" to volunteer, enthusiastic enough to stimulate an "I" to get involved, and convincing enough to get a "C" to respond. Leadership is the "S'"s most difficult task, but they can be excellent leaders if they learn to be assertive.

Because they cringe at the thought of pioneering, they should become involved in projects that stretch their "comfort zone." Learning how to adapt and respond to new stresses can be helpful. They have the potential to turn into turtles, retreating into their shells to protect themselves from the possible danger of being bruised and bumped. Taking a public speaking course may be the ultimate challenge for them. The thought of getting up in front of people and speaking may be terrifying, but this experience can result in tremendous growth.

Moses felt unqualified to lead the children of Israel out of Egypt because he believed his ability to speak was deficient. His "S" type behavior affected his attitude. Moses had to learn that God would use him (Exodus 4:12).

Most of the "S"s' problems stem from poor self-image. Reading books and listening to cassettes about self-worth and positive thinking can be beneficial to them. Robert McGee, Zig Ziglar, and James Dobson are the best teachers on the subject I know. You can find their books in almost every Christian bookstore. Also, it may be inspirational to read biographies of great Christian leaders who felt inferior but were used by God.

"S"s should be more assertive about improving their skills, but at the same time, they need to be careful concerning the philosophy that places man in the power center of life. My biggest concern about the science of human behavior is the focus it places on the created rather than the Creator. God wants us to feel good about ourselves. I heard one lady put it this way, "God don't make no junk!" We are fearfully and wonderfully made in the image of God. And we can improve and grow. Like the caterpillar in the cocoon, we can strive to become the butterfly God created us to be.

Worm Theology

Many people see themselves as worms. They believe they are hopeless and shameful, but the Scriptures teach that we are loved, forgiven, and accepted by God through Jesus Christ. We have hope and a new identity! We need to focus on all we can be and stretch our wings. We need to expand our emotions and actions outside our personal comfort zones and learn how to fly. Fear cripples "S"s. They often refuse to try new things or take advantage of new opportunities simply because they are afraid.

God has not given us the spirit of fear (2 Timothy 1:7). Scripture states that the fear of the Lord is the beginning of wisdom (Proverbs 1:7), but this fear is a healthy respect for God's power and sovereignty, not the paralyzing fear of failure, rejection, or the unknown. "S"s need to rise above their emotions to experience the satisfaction of meeting challenges.

Instead of refusing a challenge completely, take small steps. Don't be pushed into big challenges. For example, instead of setting a final goal for weight loss, determine an amount per week and eventually reach the goal.

The fear of failure coupled with the fear of the unknown is more than most "S"s want to tackle. By eliminating their mountain of fear and replacing it with rolling hills of desire, they can deal with anything. By focusing on the power of God and not concentrating on their own weakness, these normally shy people can do anything anyone else can do. Philippians 4:13 promises, "I can do all things through Christ who strengthens me."

Practical Application for "C"s

The best advice for "C"s is to be willing to settle for less than perfection. Their constant inquiries can be nerve racking; their need for answers causes stress in their relationships. Recognizing their need to fully understand will help others cope with their inquisitiveness. Ask: "Why do you ask, 'Why?'?" This question forces them to think through their question and perhaps answer it for themselves.

God challenges us with the question, "Who art thou that repliest against God, can the thing formed say to him that formed it, 'Why hast thou made me thus?'" (Romans 9:20). God knows all the answers. As mortals, we can never know as He knows. We see through a foggy glass (1 Corinthians 13:12) and cannot understand all the mysteries of God. "C"s need to rest in the fact that God knows.

It is more important to know God than to know anything else. Many of us want His blessings, but our primary motivation should be to know Him. We will never know everything, but we can know Him more intimately day by day.

Know-It-All's

"C"s usually aren't being disrespectful when they question. They just want explanations. Their drive to comprehend causes them to appear rebellious. Actually, they just want to go by the book, but if they don't understand, they can be negative and condemning. Stimulate them to think through situations on their own and allow them to use their initiative to be competent. Reason goes a long way with them, but typically, explanations create more questions for them to ask. Patience is a great virtue in dealing with them.

They tend to be more task-oriented than other people. Feelings aren't as important to them, so they may say or do things that seem to be cold and uncaring. Don't try to appeal to their emotions. Appeal to reason. Recognize that they tend to be moody when they are deep in thought. They usually aren't mad or upset; they just act like it! Give them some room. They may misunderstand and demonstrate confusion by expressing displeasure.

Stinging Words

These naturally critical people can be very caustic. Under pressure they can shoot straight, however, they avoid conflict whenever possible. When they feel threatened, they attack. They say what they think, and think about what they say, so they are often right on target. This characteristic of "telling it like it is" often gets them into trouble because most people don't like to hear the truth. They need to learn how to speak the truth in love and season their speech with sensitivity.

The Bible has a lot to say about our use of words. James 3:5-8 tells us that the tongue is small but powerful. It cannot be tamed. 1 Peter 3:10 admonishes us to refrain our tongues from evil. Constant criticism and fault-finding damage people, and a negative attitude is an insult to God's grace and goodness. Christians ought to be the most encouraging and positive people on earth.

Because they tend to worry more than others, it is important that they be surrounded by optimistic people. Don't concern them with problems. They have a knack for finding problems without our showing them! Nehemiah 8:10 states, "The joy of the Lord is our strength." True joy is not found in understanding everything or having an answer for everything. We are to pursue truth, but settling the questions of life is not our responsibility. Correctness should not be our main concern; glorifying God should be. We please and represent Him best when we contend for the faith without being contentious.

"C"s are party poopers. They dump cold water on a hot idea faster than anyone, but what they say is often very insightful. It is important to learn to listen to their advice even though they may be critical and negative. Be careful not to miss their wisdom because you don't like their attitude. Others' responses to their concerns affect their participation. Many sit and stew, contributing nothing because they were criticized for being negative.

They need to be more positive. Occasionally they need to search for the pot of gold at the end of the rainbow instead of finding the pitfalls along the way. They should whistle, sing, smile more, and they will see how much better life can be. Philippians 4:8 challenges everyone (but especially "C"s!) to think about things that are true and pure, on things that are lovely and of good report. They need to guard their thoughts. I can imagine them thinking, "How corny! How absolutely ridiculous!" That's exactly what I mean. Their initial response is usually negative. They can take this advice and improve the quality of their lives and the lives of those around them who are tired of their gloom and despair.

These critical, observant people are usually accurate in their negative appraisals, but most people don't want friends who are always right! They want friends who will forgive and forget. Friends who pick each other up, not tear each other down.

Developing People Skills

"C"s can develop their social skills by becoming involved in social activities or taking up a hobby that involves others. Finding activities which force them to relate and express their feelings will help them to become more sensitive. Above all, they should avoid their natural tendency toward depression by learning to control their feelings of inadequacy or incompetence. They need to relax and learn how to enjoy life. They don't always have to understand or explain everything.

These cautious people tend to be very competent, but they don't care much about friendships. They are not people-oriented, but some of them feel very lonely. Perhaps a lack of friends is the result of being too negative and critical of others. Proverbs 18:24 teaches us that to have friends, we must be friendly. "C"s need to develop their people skills. If they do, "C"s can be the best friends anyone has because they will always tell the truth. They aren't fakes.

In the flesh, they are difficult people to love, but in the Spirit, they can provide brilliant insights which build up instead of tear down. Their greatest challenge is to be more sensitive and tolerant of others. They must keep in mind that God, the Omnipotent One, loves and cares for all people. Spirit controlled "C"s will be competent but comforting; cautious but kind; careful but considerate of others.

Understanding our personalities is only half the knowledge we need to learn why we do what we do. In the next section we're going to look at Understanding Spiritual Gifts. It is imperative to understanding our natural and supernatural giftedness.

Part 3

Understanding Spiritual Gifts

13

Understanding Spiritual Gifts

Yₒu are gifted naturally with a specific personality. God has also gifted you with supernatural spiritual motivations. Spiritual gifts are entrusted to us by God at the moment of our conversion to Christ. Spiritual gifts are supernatural motivations given to every believer. Everyone doesn't receive the same gift. Just as many parts of the human body work together as one, so spiritual gifts are given to the body of Christ to serve as one. In Romans 12:3, Paul teaches, "Don't think more highly of yourself than you ought," because God made each part of the body to function separately, yet we are dependent upon the rest of the body.

God designed spiritual gifts to equip Christians for more effective ministry. There are at least nine motivational gifts in operation today. These nine gifts are featured because of their functional and practical use.

Eph. 4:11-13 teaches us about our spiritual gifts. In this passage we learn God gave gifts to Christians, and he gave gifted Christians to the church "for the work of the ministry, edifying of the body and unity of the faith." There are many gifts listed in the

Bible, but we're going to concentrate on only nine of them. This is not to conclude that the other gifts are not important, but the aim of this study is to discover our giftedness in a practical and functional way.

Some of the many gifts in Scripture are similar to others, such as, the gifts of helps, hospitality, and serving. They are described in similar terms. To avoid redundancy and complexity, we're going to combine these into one: "ministry / serving." The gifts of ruling, administration, and leadership are also similar. For the sake of time and space, we will blend these into the gift of "ruling / administration."

There are unique gifts found in Scripture, such as, "martyrdom" in Rev. 2:13. (I really don't think anyone wants to discover he has that gift!) There's also the gift of "celibacy" described in 1 Cor. 7 & 8, but I don't know of many single adults who would like to identify with this gift. I'm not saying these gifts are not biblical, but for the sake of practicality, we're not going focus on them.

The gifts of tongues and healing are controversial, so we are going to exclude them from our study. Our purpose is not to solve the theological debate that has existed for centuries. We simply want to solve the practical and functional problems of the church. We're only focusing on "where do I fit best in the body of Christ, plus how can I avoid and resolve conflicts once I get involved in ministry?"

Completing the *Spiritual Gifts Profile* will identify your supernatural giftedness. The assessment is not a test; it is an inventory. Once you have identified your primary spiritual gifts, you will understand better why you feel, think, and act in the context of ministry.

The following is a sample of the *Spiritual Gifts Profile* questionnaire. Don't try to complete it, because the scoring instructions are not included.

To order a *Discover Your Giftedness Profile* write to: Uniquely You Resources, P. O. Box 490, Blue Ridge, GA 30513 or to order call: (800) 501-0490; for information call: (706) 632-8411; or to fax: (706) 632-3484.

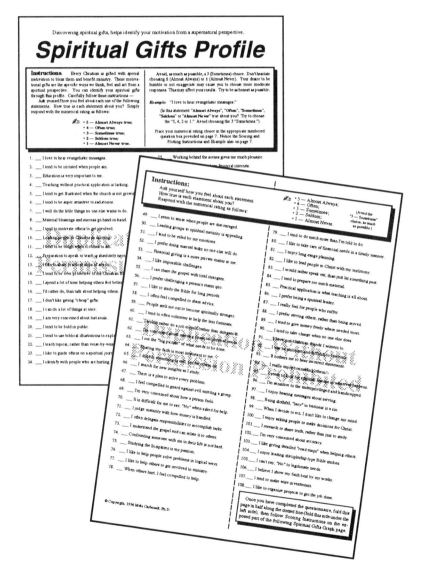

This is a sample of a spiritual gifts graph. Once you have completed your *Spiritual Gifts Profile*, you should focus on understanding your three highest gifts.

The higher the plotting point the more that gift will describe your behavior.

You should also identify your lowest gift to see if there is something you should also learn.

Evangelism	Prophecy	Teaching	Exhortation	Pastor / Shepherd	Showing Mercy	Ministry / Serving	Giving	Administ. / Ruling
A	**B**	**C**	**D**	**E**	**F**	**G**	**H**	**I**
60	60	60	60	60	60	60	60	60
59	59	59	59	59	59	59	59	59
58	58	58	58	58	58	58	58	58
57	57	57	57	57	57	57	57	57
56	56	56	56	56	56	56	56	56
55	55	55	55	55	55	55	55	55
54	54	54	54	54	54	54	54	54
53	53	53	53	53	53	53	53	53
52	52	52	52	52	52	52	52	52
51	51	51	51	51	51	51	51	51
50	50	50	50	50	50	50	50	50
49	49	49	49	49	49	49	49	49
48	48	48	48	48	48	48	48	48
47	47	47	47	47	47	47	47	47
46	46	46	46	46	46	46	46	46
45	45	45	45	45	45	45	45	45
44	44	44	44	44	44	44	44	44
43	43	43	43	43	43	43	43	43
42	42	42	42	42	42	42	42	42
41	41	41	41	41	41	41	41	41
40	40	40	40	40	40	40	40	40
39	39	39	39	39	39	39	39	39
38	38	38	38	38	38	38	38	38
37	37	37	37	37	37	37	37	37
36	36	36	36	36	36	36	36	36
35	35	35	35	35	35	35	35	35
34	34	34	34	34	34	34	34	34
33	33	33	33	33	33	33	33	33
32	32	32	32	32	32	32	32	32
31	31	31	31	31	31	31	31	31
30	30	30	30	30	30	30	30	30
29	29	29	29	29	29	29	29	29
28	28	28	28	28	28	28	28	28
27	27	27	27	27	27	27	27	27
26	26	26	26	26	26	26	26	26
25	25	25	25	25	25	25	25	25
24	24	24	24	24	24	24	24	24
23	23	23	23	23	23	23	23	23
22	22	22	22	22	22	22	22	22
21	21	21	21	21	21	21	21	21
20	20	20	20	20	20	20	20	20
19	19	19	19	19	19	19	19	19
18	18	18	18	18	18	18	18	18
17	17	17	17	17	17	17	17	17
16	16	16	16	16	16	16	16	16
15	15	15	15	15	15	15	15	15
14	14	14	14	14	14	14	14	14
13	13	13	13	13	13	13	13	13
12	12	12	12	12	12	12	12	12
11	11	11	11	11	11	11	11	11
10	10	10	10	10	10	10	10	10
9	9	9	9	9	9	9	9	9

Keep in mind, this assessment doesn't measure passion, calling, or anointing. You may be serving in a ministry that doesn't match your giftedness. This is not necessarily a problem. It may indicate maturity and a willingness to do whatever God calls you to do. We must always be flexible to respond to the Lord's leading, rather than respond only to our feelings and thoughts. God often asks people to do things they are not gifted to do.

The following descriptions are simple overviews of the spiritual gifts listed in Romans 12:3-8 and Ephesians 4:11-12. Read each one and review the results of your *Spiritual Gifts Profile* to identify your specific spiritual motivations.

Focus on your three primary gifts from your graph. Read through all the following descriptions to see if there are other gifts that may explain your passion or calling.

Evangelism —

Christians with the gift of evangelism feel compelled to win souls. They seem to have the ability to communicate the gospel very effectively. Their concern for witnessing to a lost and dying world is evident. They desire to be involved in ministries to reach people for Christ. The gift of evangelism motivates them to want nearly every message they hear to include the gospel and an invitation to trust Christ. Missions and outreach are important to them. Their goal is to be ready to give an answer to every person they meet. Conversations seem to often turn toward eternal values. The worth of souls and the task of evangelism are most important to the evangelist's motivation.

Prophecy —

Prophets today are not exactly like prophets of old. Old Testament prophets spoke the literal Word of God. Today people with the gift of prophecy seem to have the same seriousness and straight forward attitude toward truth, but they apply the truth of the Bible instead of uttering it initially like the Old Testament prophets. Today's prophets like to share truth, regardless of others' responses. They are motivated to confront anyone with what they believe is right. When controlled by the Holy Spirit, the gift of prophecy is a powerful tool to reprove, rebuke, and exhort others. Prophets often find themselves pointing the way, declaring specific truth or standing up for something significant.

Teaching —

Christians with the gift of teaching prefer to explain why things are true and study passages of Scripture in depth. While the prophet declares truth, the teacher explains the reasons it is true. Interested in research, those with the gift of teaching like to dig into seemingly insignificant details, and they enjoy presenting what they discover. They are sometimes oblivious of other's needs as they press toward a deeper understanding. While searching patiently and persistently, they occasionally miss the obvious. They stretch the limits of learning, setting high standards of education.

Exhortation —

Christians with the gift of exhortation find themselves encouraging others. They are compelled to give advice. As counselors, they often provide people with steps of action. While prophets declare truth and teachers clarify truth, exhorters like to tell you what to do with truth. They bless others with a strong sense of concern. They are sought out as counselors because they are so good at encouraging others. People find exhorters to be friendly, understanding, and practical people who enjoy using their communication skills to share specific insights.

Pastor / Shepherd —

The gift of pastor / shepherd is obvious in those who really enjoy leading others in serving the Lord. Unlike the gift of serving / ministry, this gift involves the motivation to lead. Pastor / shepherds are compelled to encourage others to work together for the body's sake. Influencing others to work together is important. They emphasize harmony as they stress a need for team participation. Laymen and women can also have the gift of pastor / shepherd. They see their service as one of maturing others, often in the context of small groups. With a motivation to unite the ministry, they feel strong about the spiritual health of those they lead.

Showing Mercy —

Christians with the gift of showing mercy demonstrate genuine sensitivity to others' suffering. They are compelled to help people in pain and are concerned more with the person than the reason for the suffering. Focusing on the feelings of those who hurt, merciful people strongly desire to minister by "being there" when people really need them. Sympathizing and empathizing are their specialties. While others may care more about why, what, when or how, those with the gift of showing mercy are interested in *who* needs tender loving care.

Ministry / Serving —

When you think of Christians who serve faithfully behind the scenes, those with the gift of ministry / serving come to mind. They are interested in blessing others to serve the Lord. They love to help others. They are motivated by a strong sense of need, and they feel like "someone has to do it." Caring and concerned, they often find themselves doing what no one else likes to do. They are flexible and adapt to many challenges. They simply enjoy helping others and meeting needs.

Giving —

Givers tend to be seriously concerned about financial matters. The gift of giving also involves the "gift of getting." Givers are sensitive to how money is spent and saved. Those with the gift of giving don't always give to the wheel that squeaks the loudest but to the wheel that truly needs the most grease. They often have unique financial insights and serve especially well on boards responsible for maintaining budgets. They tend to be conscientious and conservative. People with the gift of giving may not be conspicuous in a crowd, but their genuine interest in wise stewardship will be.

Administration / Ruling —

The gift of administration / ruling is seen in those who either like to organize or delegate to others. These people are compelled by a strong sense of duty, and they like to find things for people to do. Unlike the gift of service / ministry, the gift of administration / ruling focuses on team participation. They see the big picture and work to keep everyone on track. These people are always personally organized. They are adept at evaluating what needs to be done, then designing systems or giving responsibilities to those who can get the job done.

Begin thinking how your supernatural motivations (spiritual gifts) affect your natural motivations (personality) and how, together, they relate to ministry. God doubly blessed you with these motivations to glorify Himself. God gifted you for the "edifying of the body," Eph. 4:12. Since edification is encouragement, you will never be more encouraged in life, than when you exercise your giftedness. You will also encourage and bless others, as you allow God to use you.

The following is an simple overview of each spiritual gift.

Evangelism —

In a word: Dynamic
Overuse: Zeal
Goal: Build disciples, not statistics.
Scripture References: Eph. 4:11 & Acts 8:5-6

Prophecy —

In a word: Bold
Overuse: Fighter
Goal: Declare truth, don't divide Christians.
Scripture References: 1 Cor. 12:10, 28 & 14:3

Teaching —

In a word: In-depth
Overuse: Digs too deep
Goal: Reveal truth, don't exhaust it.
Scripture References: 1 Cor. 12:28 and Acts 20:20-21

Exhortation —

In a word: Encourager
Overuse: Talks too much
Goal: Apply truth, don't create expectations.
Scripture References: Rom. 12:8 and Acts 13:43

Pastor / Shepherd —

In a word: Initiator
Overuse: Expects too much
Goal: Lead by example, not manipulation.
Scripture References: Eph. 4:11 and 1 Pet. 5:1-3

Showing Mercy —

In a word: Caring
Overuse: Too sensitive
Goal: Wise insights, not foolish responses.
Scripture References: Rom. 12:8 and Acts 9:36

Ministry / Serving —

In a word: Selfless
Overuse: Takes on too much
Goal: Be a servant, not a martyr.
Scripture References: Rom 12:7 and 2 Tim. 1:16-18

Giving —

In a word: Steward
Overuse: The power of money
Goal: Sincere stewardship, not financial control.
Scripture References: Rom. 12:8 and Mark 12:41-44

Administration / Ruling—

In a word: Leader
Overuse: Takes Advantage of Others' Trust
Goal: Strong leadership, not manipulating flock.
Scripture References: Rom. 12:8 and Titus 1:5

To illustrate the importance of understanding how specific spiritual gifts may relate to other spiritual gifts, imagine nine people, each with a different spiritual gift, coming together for a Benevolence Committee meeting. They have met because someone in the church needs $90 to pay his electric bill. How do you think each Benevolence Committee member will predictably respond based upon his or her spiritual gift?

The member with the gift of evangelism will first ask if the person is saved or not? The individual with the gift of prophecy will probably demand that the member get a job! The person with the gift of teaching will want to research the Scriptures to find exactly what to do in this circumstance.

The individual with the gift of exhortation will want to give specific steps of action to encourage the member concerning his need. The one with the gift of ministry / serving may offer to baby-sit while the member goes job hunting. The committee member with the gift of showing mercy will probably plea to first pay the bill and then decide what to do next.

The one with the gift of pastor / shepherd will want to get the member involved in some kind of discipleship program or Bible study. The person with the gift of giving will want to put the member on a budget or be sure he gets financial counseling. And the member with the gift of administration / ruling will demand the member be placed under the authority of the committee in order to guarantee it doesn't happen again.

This illustration is a little exaggerated, but you can begin to see the importance of understanding other people's motivations and responses based upon their spiritual gifts. Whenever you work with people, think about how your personality and spiritual gifts relate to them. Once you have identified your personality type and spiritual gifts, you can learn how personalities affect spiritual gifts, and vise versa. Discovering your combination of personalities and spiritual gifts is exciting!

14

Combining Personalities With Spiritual Gifts

Relating our natural motivations (personality types) to our supernatural motivations (spiritual gift types) can be enlightening. Most personality types relate to specific spiritual gift types. Such as, individuals with the gifts of serving or showing mercy often have "S" type personalities.

"D" and "C" type personalities often have the gifts of prophecy or administration / ruling. "Exhorters" are often "I" or "S" types. The gift of teaching corresponds best to "C" behavior.

Sometimes God combines a specific personality with an unrelated spiritual gift. I used to say, *"I never met a prophet with an "S" type personality."* After much prayer and study, I noticed Jeremiah was the *"weeping prophet."* He perceived and proclaimed truth but was also sensitive.

God is not in a box. He does what He pleases. The Lord sometimes gifts individuals with seemingly opposing endowments and enablements — differing natural and supernatural giftedness. It's not common but is normal. It will also explain why some

Christians are often confused and frustrated by their conflicting motivations.

People with the gift of prophecy are often serious and hard on those who are indifferent to right and wrong. The gift of prophecy comes across with more "D" and "C" type behavior. But the "S" type prophet can be very sensitive and stable. The "S" prophet is motivated by a strong sense of loyalty and protection of those they love.

Most people have spiritual gifts that relate to their personality types. But regardless of whether your spiritual gifts and personality type relate to each other, God has a purpose for gifting you the way He has. Be open to the unique way God wants to use you.

Recognizing your uniqueness can help you find your place of service. Everyone is somebody in His body. Scripture is full of admonitions that encourage your getting involved.

Discovering your giftedness helps you understand how God has designed you to glorify Himself.

Identifying your unique combination can be liberating. Some believers have uncommon (not "abnormal") combinations. Unfortunately, most Bible teachers today describe spiritual gifts in temperament terms. For example, the gift of showing mercy is always described in "S" terms — sensitive, sweet, and soft. But there are those with the gift of showing mercy and a "D" type personality. They demand that everyone shows mercy!

The following are combinations of D, I, S and C type personalities with nine spiritual gifts.

First, identify which letter (D, I, S or C) best describes your personality type. This can be done by finding the highest plotting point/s on Graphs 1 & 2 in your *Spiritual Gifts Profile*.

Then notice your most obvious spiritual gift/s. Do this by finding the highest plotting point/s in your Spiritual Gifts Profile.

There are 36 combinations of personality types and spiritual gifts. Find the description/s of your combinations. You may have several combinations to identify.

Consider the insights that most describe you and disregard those that are not like you. Keep in mind, you are a blend of behaviors and gifts. Prayerfully study each description, asking God to control your personality and spiritual gift/s for His glory.

Study this book to also find where God can use you in ministry. Discovering your personality and spiritual gift/s should result in maturity and involvement in the Body of Christ.

"D" Type Personalities With The Gift of Evangelism

Dynamic and demanding type Christians with the gift of evangelism can be extremely effective. They are self-starters with a sense of urgency. But their driving concern to win souls can make them too pushy. "D"-evangelists should be more gentle and patient. Determined to get the job done, they often feel like everyone should be involved in evangelism. Direct with their presentations, they like sermons that explain the gospel and offer invitations to trust Christ. "D"-evangelists are dedicated to *"making Him known."*

"I" Type Personalities With The Gift of Evangelism

Influencing type Christians with the gift of evangelism are most enthusiastic about soul winning. They are also very contagious — cheerleaders for Christ. Interested in people, they are "natural-born" witnesses. "I"-evangelists make sharing the gospel look so easy. Because of their strong desire to impress, they may care equally about what people think of them and leading others to Christ. They must constantly remember God gifted them to shine for Him, not self. "I"-evangelists can win many souls to Christ.

"S" Type Personalities With The Gift of Evangelism

Sweet and soft type Christians with the gift of evangelism are the most gentle witnesses. They steadily share the gospel. They don't like to force issues. They tend to be too nice. Scoffers often waste "S"-evangelists' time. Knowing they will go the extra mile, some people take advantage. Avoiding confrontation, these stable types prefer "friendship evangelism." But their motivation to win souls often overcomes their natural reluctance to speak out. "S"-evangelists enjoy bringing people to Jesus without a lot of fanfare.

"C" Type Personalities With The Gift of Evangelism

Cautious and compliant type Christians with the gift of evangelism are the most thorough witnesses. They like to go point-by-point, convincing people to understand every detail. They try to have an answer for every question. But they can overwhelm with too many facts. "C"-evangelists are often more concerned with the task, rather than the person in need. As competent individuals, they need to be more flexible and friendly. "C"-evangelists can turn doubt into a fascinating opportunity for Christ.

"D" Type Personalities With The Gift of Prophecy

Demanding type Christians with the gift of prophecy are fearless concerning truth. Determined to preserve purity, they tend to dominate others. As protectors of righteousness, they proclaim truth without concern for what anyone thinks. They often feel like they have the divine right to be pushy. "D"-prophets are so driving, they often offend others. They need to be more gentle, rather than always striving to expose error. They should be more sensitive to the feelings of others. "D"-prophets are the most effective declarers of truth.

"I" Type Personalities With The Gift of Prophecy

Influencing type Christians with the gift of prophecy make great communicators of truth. They articulate correctness with persuasion. They tend to overuse enthusiasm and emotions to convince others. Able to induce action or reaction, they need to guard against verbal abuse. Proclaiming truth, "I"-prophets should season their speech with sugar. Making great impressions, they must remember Who they represent, not what they defend. "I"-prophets are inspiring protectors of the faith.

"S" Type Personalities With The Gift of Prophecy

Sensitive type Christians with the gift of prophecy are shy but serious concerning truth. They seem to be soft, but their concern makes them persuaders. Motivated to proclaim truth, they tend to be gentle, but strong. "S"-prophets seem to struggle with their concern for individuals and standing for correctness. This balance makes them surprisingly effective. People are often impressed when their shyness turns into firmness. They need to be careful about extremes. "S"-prophets are like sleeping giants when it comes to truth.

"C" Type Personalities With The Gift of Prophecy

Calculating type Christians with the gift of prophecy are cautious and competent. They tend to be conscientious. They can be too critical of those who compromise the truth. Often convincing, they tend to be confrontational. Their concern for compliance often makes them unbending. "C" prophets are insightful, but can be insensitive to what others feel. They would increase effectiveness with greater interest in others, rather than always being right. As protectors of truth, "C"-prophets are able to see and share correctness.

"D" Type Personalities With The Gift of Teaching

Demanding type Christians with the gift of teaching are dedicated students and driving instructors. They like challenging research in order to convince others. They tend to be too forceful. "D"-teachers make strong disciplinarians. Often domineering, they need to be more gentle with their insights. Digging deep while getting to the point can be frustrating. They should balance dedication to teaching with more people-orientation. "D"-teachers can get the job done when it comes to explaining why something is true.

"I" Type Personalities With The Gift of Teaching

Inspiring type Christians with the gift of teaching are most interesting. They tell the best stories. They use clear illustrations. Their verbal skills create fascinating studies. But they tend to have lengthy classes. "I"-teachers need to be more time-conscientious. They may also stretch the text to make a point. Concerned about what others think, they often make good impressions. They can become prideful because of their tremendous ability to communicate. "I"-teachers are some of the most interesting instructors.

"S" Type Personalities With The Gift of Teaching

Stable type Christians with the gift of teaching are systematic researchers. They like to teach steadily, step-by-step. Their simple, but insightful instruction often lacks excitement. They need to be more animated. "S"-teachers make faithful and loyal friends, but often resist conflict. They should strive to be more interested in results, than relationships and revelation. Concerned about harmony and accuracy, they can be too sweet and slow to share why something is true. You can count on "S"-teachers for the thorough explanation.

"C" Type Personalities With The Gift of Teaching

Compliant type Christians with the gift of teaching are controlled by the quest for truth. They make great researchers. Determined to discover in-depth truth, they can overdo their lessons. They can become too factual. People seem to find "C"-teachers competent, but boring. They can lack enthusiasm and warmth. They should focus more on practical application. As critical thinkers, "C"-teachers can sound sarcastic. When sensitive, excited and patient, "C"-teachers make great instructors.

"D" Type Personalities With The Gift of Exhortation

Decisive type Christians with the gift of exhortation are persistent encouragers. They tend to dominate conversations with practical steps-of-action. They like to share advice. "D"-exhorters are driven to control the situation in order to encourage. They need to be more flexible and sensitive. People can't always do or feel what "D"-exhorters want. They tend to have a plan for every problem. Often impatient, they can be too pushy. Letting others share their ideas, while determined to encourage others, makes them extremely effective.

"I" Type Personalities With The Gift of Exhortation

Inspiring type Christians with the gift of exhortation make enthusiastic encouragers. They impress others with their advice. But they can be too optimistic. They often create high expectations. They need to be more realistic. "I"-exhorters should guard against using their verbal skills to manipulate others. They may try to influence others to do more than humanly possible. They should listen more and speak less. Interested in others, they often induce positive responses. "I"-exhorters communicate encouragement best.

"S" Type Personalities With The Gift of Exhortation

Sensitive type Christians with the gift of exhortation are sweet encouragers. They share simple and slow steps-of-action to help others. They often wait for others to ask for advice. They are not pushy. They love to stabilize bad situations with practical ideas. "S"-exhorters can be too shy. They may wait instead of aggressively confronting an issue. They need to be more assertive. Their concern for others often makes them too nice. They may need to show "tough love." "S"-exhorters are security-oriented encouragers.

"C" Type Personalities With The Gift of Exhortation

Calculating type Christians with the gift of exhortation are precise encouragers. They often know just what to say. Their practical steps-of-action tend to be concise. They make competent counselors with specific insights. But they can be too hard on people. "C"-exhorters can see what needs to be done, but fail at communicating love. They should be more sensitive to the failures of others. Having patience and kindness will increase effectiveness. They should not be so critical. "C"-exhorters can make great problem-solvers.

"D" Type Personalities With The Gift Pastor / Shepherd

Demanding type Christians with the gift of pastor/shepherd tend to be ministry driven. Seeing the big picture, they are compelled to lead others. Their domineering ways can be misunderstood as dictatorial. They may be genuinely dedicated to shepherding others, but have strong feelings about what things should be done. Slowly working through people will make them more effective. Often taking charge, they seem to control others. Their concern for the flock is evident. "D"-pastor/shepherds make great visionaries.

"I" Type Personalities With The Gift of Pastor / Shepherd

Inspiring type Christians with the gift of pastor/shepherd are impressive. Their influence makes people enjoy working and worshiping. They can be extremely successful and must guard against pride. People look up to "I"-pastor/shepherds. Able to persuade, they need to be more cautious what they promote. They love to minister and encourage others to do so. Often concerned more about what others think, they need to guard against using people to build their ministries. They can be best at using their ministry to build people.

"S" Type Personalities With The Gift of Pastor / Shepherd

Submissive type Christians with the Gift of pastor/shepherd are selfless servants. They enjoy building relationships that result in ministries. They shepherd by example, not demand. They can be too nice. Often more caring than confrontational, they may need to be more assertive. Concerned about the ministry, they should be more enthusiastic. Shyness often hinders their leadership. People appreciate their interest in ministry, but some may want them to be more decisive. "S"-pastor/shepherds make gentle leaders.

"C" Type Personalities With The Gift of Pastor / Shepherd

Conscientious type Christians with the gift of pastor/shepherd are methodical. They like to go-by-the-book. They don't like to take risks and venture away from what they know works. They may need to be more open to innovation. They strive for correctness. Purity in the group is important to "C"-pastor/shepherds. Enthusiasm will encourage more to minister. Often conservative, they tend to be picky. Detailed assignments for everyone can often be overdone. "C"-pastor/shepherds are competent church leaders.

"D" Type Personalities With The Gift of Showing Mercy

Determined type Christians with the gift of showing mercy are rare, but dedicated to helping others feel better. Their domineering ways tend to conflict with their desire to sympathize with others. They can be decisive, while merciful and kind. "D"-showing mercy types are unique individuals who tend to demand that everyone display a caring spirit. Their driving personalities can be misunderstood as insensitive, while showing mercy is their motivation. They should guard their dominance with loving hearts. They press the need to care.

"I" Type Personalities With The Gift of Showing Mercy

Inspiring type Christians with the gift of showing mercy influence others to care more. They use verbal skills to generate excitement for the cause of demonstrating love. Interested in people, they induce strong feelings of concern. They can be too emotional. "I"-showing mercy types can overdo their influence. Some people may think their concern is all show. They like to impress others with their kindness. They may need to calm down and be more humble. When it comes to evident sensitivity, "I"-showing mercy types are tops.

"S" Type Personalities With The Gift of Showing Mercy

Sensitive type Christians with the gift of showing mercy are most loving. They are sweet servants always ready to help. They specialize in times of suffering. "S"-showing mercy types may be so concerned that they miss opportunities to teach lessons. They can also be fooled by insincere cries for help. They may need to be more assertive with those who use their pain as excuses. They should be more demanding. They may need to share truth, rather than always listening. When people hurt, "S"-showing mercy types shine.

"C" Type Personalities With The Gift of Showing Mercy

Compliant type Christians with the gift of showing mercy are extremely concerned about others. They see needs no one else sees. They tend to know exactly what to say. They are careful not to miss opportunities to help, but can be critical of those who don't get involved. "C"-showers of mercy may try to analyze why people hurt. Their conservative care is often appreciated. They need to be optimistic. Enthusiasm and inspiration are often lacking. "C"-showers of mercy are competent individuals who really care about suffering.

"D" Type Personalities With The Gift of Ministry / Serving

Driving type Christians with the gift of ministry stay busy for Christ. They tend to work hard behind the scenes, doing whatever needs to be done. They can be impatient with those who don't help. Determined to minister, they tend to dominate and intimidate others to also serve. "D"-servants are task-oriented individuals working tirelessly. They may need to slow down, relax and delegate. They can become demanding and offensive. "D"-servants are dedicated to ministering and helping others. They are self-sacrificing doers of the Word.

"I" Type Personalities With The Gift of Ministry / Serving

Inspiring type Christians with the gift of ministry are excited about serving. Their impressive enthusiasm makes others want to get involved. They can be too persuasive and impatient. "I"-servants are extremely effective in inducing action. They tend to oversell and manipulate. Influencing others, they should guard their verbal skills when the job needs to get done. "I"-servants tend to work longer than necessary, because they talk too much. Creating an exciting atmosphere of service is their specialty.

"S" Type Personalities With The Gift of Ministry / Serving

Steady type Christians with the gift of ministry are every church's dream — the backbone of ministry. If anything needs to get done, they faithfully serve without recognition. They are not bossy, but should be more assertive. People take advantage of "S"-servants. They should be more aggressive in seeking help. Always sensitive to the feelings of others makes them sought out. But sometimes they solve problems for those who may need to feel the pressure of their irresponsibility. "S"-servants are the most stable servants.

"C" Type Personalities With The Gift of Ministry / Serving

Competent type Christians with the gift of ministry are detail-oriented. They don't like loose ends. If anything needs to be done right, they are perfect for the job. "C"-servants tend to be difficult to work with. They can be too picky. They need to be more friendly and cooperative. Often feeling like they are the only ones who ever do anything, they need to appreciate others more. Positive attitudes and enthusiasm are recommended but difficult for "C"-servants. They can be the hardest working and compliant servants.

"D" Type Personalities With The Gift of Giving

Domineering type Christians with the gift of giving are serious about financial matters. They can be very successful in business. They also have the "gift of getting." They tend to use money to control others. Demanding how finances are used, they can be extremely picky with budgets. They seldom give to the wheel that squeaks the loudest. They are either unbending or influencing concerning financial decisions. They either discourage or encourage others with their money and/or advice. They can make great financial counselors.

"I" Type Personalities With The Gift of Giving

Impressing type Christians with the gift of giving are enthusiastic about stewardship. They like to encourage everyone to be givers. They make great promoters, but can kill projects because of financial concerns. "I"-givers are more optimistic than others.

They can be too positive. Their faith is evident in giving, but can become prideful. They like to tell everyone how to give more. When discouraged, they may use their verbal skills and financial credibility to influence others. "I"-givers are most excited when it involves finances.

"S" Type Personalities With The Gift of Giving

Security-oriented type Christians with the gift of giving are not risk takers. They are submissive (willing) givers. They may lack the vision necessary to take on challenging projects. Sensitive to individual needs, they help others behind the scenes. They are private about giving. "S"-givers can be too helpful. They need to guard their sincere desire to serve with a stronger determination to do what is right. They can be taken advantage of. They tend to be the most sacrificing. "S"-givers are stable financial planners who avoid financial disasters.

"C" Type Personalities With The Gift of Giving

Compliant type Christians with the gift of giving are cautious. They move conservatively. They seldom make quick financial decisions. They don't like pressure. Vision and growth are often stifled because of pessimism. "C"-givers seldom make investment mistakes, but may miss great opportunities. They need to be more positive. People often think they are critical. They should be more friendly. Respected by others, they should use their competence to help, rather than find fault. They can be valuable in financial planning.

"D" Type Personalities With The Gift of Administration / Ruling

Demanding type Christians with the gift of administration / ruling are strong leaders. They like to tell others what to do. They often see what needs to be done and delegate the work to others. They can be too bossy. "D"-administrators tend to see the big picture, but lack warmth to get others to help without pressure. They can intimidate and offend if not careful. Often concerned more about tasks, than people, they need to be sensitive and loving. "D"-administrators can be gifted leaders who press forward to do great things for God.

"I" Type Personalities With The Gift of Administration / Ruling

Influencing type Christians with the gift of administration / ruling are optimistic leaders. Their positive enthusiasm encourages others to get involved. They can be overly excited. They tend to talk people into doing things they don't want to do. They impress others with their friendliness and verbal skills. "I"-administrators need to guard against manipulating. They should serve by example. They often take on more than they can handle, disappointing those who expect a lot from them. But they can accomplish much through people.

"S" Type Personalities With The Gift of Administration / Ruling

Submissive type Christians with the gift of administration / ruling are concerned about getting tasks done in steady and stable ways. They need to be more assertive and aggressive. "S"-administrators can be too sacrificing. They are faithful in whatever they do, but need to inspire others to help. They can be quiet leaders, challenging others by example. They tend to be shy.

Sometimes, they surprise others with their serious concern to accomplish tasks. "S"-administrators are achievers who like to work through small groups.

"C" Type Personalities With The Gift of Administration / Ruling

Cautious type Christians with the gift of administration/ruling are competent taskmasters. They see a need and organize others to meet that need. They enjoy doing things completely right the first time. They tend to be picky. They would increase effectiveness with more warmth and team participation. Working through people and creating enthusiastic atmospheres can he helpful. They should avoid being critical of what others do. "C"-administrators are best able to get groups to do the right things.

Once you have identified your combination personality and spiritual gifts, you can understand better how God has gifted you to fulfill your destiny. He gifted you with specific motivations to use and bless you for His glory. The following chapter will help you discover where you fit best.

15

Where Do You Fit?

Many Christians are miserable because they don't understand how God wants to exercise His gifts through them. Divine enjoyment only comes when we exercise God's grace in our lives. Grace is not only "undeserved mercy." It is also the "ability and power to do God's will." It is so exciting when we discover that God has given each of us the power, a measure of grace, to glorify Him!

God typically uses people in specific areas based upon their giftedness, however, God uses all personalities and spiritual gifts in great ways. No personality or spiritual gift is better than others.

Once you identify your giftedness, your ministry involvement can be based upon your personality and spiritual gifts. You will feel more comfortable and confident when you serve where you fit best. You will also be more effective since you will operate out of your strengths. The question now is: "Where do you fit best?"

Review the following insights to understand more about ministry involvement from perspective of your personality, then review your involvement from a spiritual gifts perspective.

Involvement From the Perspective of Personality

"D" BEHAVIOR *(Active / Task-oriented)*

Abilities: Lead, take stand, confront issue, persevere, dictate, make decisions and control.

Opportunities: Organize needed ministry, chair Stewardship Committee, head Usher's Committee, commit to specific challenge.

Warning: You want to control everyone, but you must first control yourself. Remember, to have authority, you must be under authority. Be loyal to your leaders.

Reward: Follow your spiritual leaders. Allow Christ to be the Lord of your life, then God will use you in a great way to move the ministry forward.

Prayer: *"Dear God, control my driving, demanding and dominant personality, so I can be a strong and peace-making leader for your glory."*

"I" BEHAVIOR *(Active / People-oriented)*

Abilities: Communicate, inspire, influence, make friends, optimism, enthusiasm.

Opportunities: Give public testimony, drama, social committee, greeter, encourager, lead discussion group and visitation.

Warning: You naturally outshine others, but don't serve purely through your naturally attractive personality because pride and sinful lusts will destroy your testimony.

Reward: God designed you to shine for Him. When you allow Him to shine through you, He will use you in greater ways than you ever imagined.

Prayer: *"Dear God, keep me humble to do your will, not mine. Help me give You the credit for all You have done."*

"S" BEHAVIOR   *(Passive / People-oriented)*

Abilities: Support, serve, specialize, finish what others start, work behind the scenes, do what needs to be done.

Opportunities: On call whenever needed, hospital visitation, encourage new members, office, keep records, telephoning and counseling.

Warning: Shyness hinders your opportunities to do great things for God. Be more aggressive and assertive, and be careful because people may try to take advantage of you.

Reward: Believing God's promise that you can do all things through Him who strengthens you, step out and try the difficult. You may be surprised what God can do.

Prayer: *"Dear God, I know you use the weak things to confound the mighty and I often don't feel capable of serving you, but through your grace, I will."*

"C" BEHAVIOR   *(Passive / Task-oriented)*

Abilities: Analyze, improve, discern, calculate, follow directions, do the right thing.

Opportunities: Finance Committee, long-range planning, office, record information, research, teach, organize and order curriculum.

Warning: You are naturally analytical, but this strength can turn to criticism of others too easily. Don't be pessimistic and stubborn. Increase your faith in God and trust those you follow.

Reward: Ministers need competent people to fulfill their visions. You can be a great blessing if you continually look at the possibilities, rather than impossibilities.

Prayer: *"Dear God, help me be optimistic in the midst of problems — a source of encouragement to those who find faith and victory difficult."*

Note:

You should never use your personality as an excuse to avoid doing what God commands everyone to do. For example, the Bible commands all of us to do the work of an evangelist. "D"s and "I"s may feel more comfortable talking to people about Christ, while "S"s and "C"s may not. Yet everyone should share the Good News. "S"s may feel more comfortable working behind the scenes, but God may call an "S" like Moses to lead a group. Or God may call an "I" to work behind the scenes, which is not where an "I" feels comfortable at all! We must learn to "be all things to all men that we might by all means save some."

Whatever you do, do it through Christ. Read Gal. 2:20.

Involvement From A
Spiritual Gifts Perspective

One of the best ways to grow as a Christian is to get involved in ministry. Identifying your natural and spiritual motivation will help you get plugged in. Many believers desire personal growth, but comparatively few take the initiative to find a rewarding ministry.

The following is a summary of nine spiritual gifts and how they can impact your life.

GIFT OF EVANGELISM —

Abilities: Comfortably share the gospel with results.
Opportunities: Visitation, Outreach, Missions.
Warning: Don't think everyone should be as dedicated to evangelism as you are.
Reward: Leading people to Christ glorifies God.
Prayer: *"Dear God, increase my vision for the lost, and help me understand why others do not share my burden."*

GIFT OF PROPHECY —

Abilities: Discern right from wrong / Declare truth.
Opportunities: Community / National Concern,
Finances, Steering Committee.
Warning: Don't be obnoxious or opinionated.
Reward: Helping others see truth clearly.
Prayer: *"Dear God, give me the sensitivity to show love—and the courage to share truth that may offend."*

GIFT OF TEACHING —

Abilities: Clarify truth / Insights as to why facts are true.
Opportunities: Teaching, Training, Library.
Warning: Don't neglect other responsibilities.
Reward: Knowing people learn truth.
Prayer: *"Dear God, help me to be practical, not just to impart truth.*

GIFT OF EXHORTATION —

Abilities: Share practical steps of action.
Opportunities: Counseling, Crisis Center, Evangelism.
Warning: Choose your words wisely.
Reward: Seeing people respond to your advice and helping them through problems.
Prayer: *"Dear God, use me to say what You would have me to say, not what I feel at the moment."*

GIFT OF PASTOR / SHEPHERD —

Abilities: Ministering to groups needing leadership.
Opportunities: Committee Chairperson, Visitation.
Warning: Don't get discouraged with those who don't follow.
Reward: Seeing the ministry improve.
Prayer: *"Dear God, help me be patient with those who are*

apathetic or spiritually weak."

GIFT OF SHOWING MERCY —

Abilities: Giving sympathy and/or empathy to the hurting.
Opportunities: Hospital, Benevolence, Counseling.
Warning: Don't be a sucker to everyone who needs you.
Reward: Knowing you helped those who no one else would help.
Prayer: *"Dear God, use me to not only to help people by showing love, but also sharing truth and TOUGH LOVE when necessary."*

GIFT OF MINISTRY / SERVING —

Abilities: Serving behind the scenes.
Opportunities: Nursery, Sunday School, Ushering.
Warning: Don't become weary in well-doing.
Reward: Knowing you make a difference doing what no one else may have wanted to do.
Prayer: *"Dear God, thank you for appreciating my labor of love—regardless of what others may fail to appreciate."*

GIFT OF GIVING —

Abilities: Using stewardship to further God's Kingdom.
Opportunities: Finance or Planning Committee, Office.
Warning: Don't use money to control others.
Reward: Knowing you contributed to the advancement of ministry without any personal recognition.
Prayer: *Dear God, use my success with finances to bless the ministry and others."*

GIFT OF ADMINISTRATION / RULING —

Abilities: Organizing or delegating tasks.
Opportunities: Group Leader, Office, Personnel.

Warning: Avoid demanding everyone get involved the way you want them to.

Reward: Seeing people work together to accomplish difficult tasks.

Prayer: *"Dear God, help me to be tolerant to those who don't respond like I think they should."*

God has a special place of service and blessing for every Christian. We need to find where God is working and get involved. We also need to find where God has given us a burden to serve. God sometimes gives us a burden that doesn't match our giftedness. This burden becomes a passion that overrides our giftedness. We may not be gifted with communication skills, but our passion to help someone or a group can cause us to get involved.

Our natural motivations can also be overridden by our supernatural spiritual gifts. For example, you may have the gift of showing mercy, but your "D" personality may cause you to demand that others also show mercy. Your interest in ministry may seem more sweet and sensitive, but you have a drive and determination to get the job done. You may feel compelled to serve in a ministry that shows mercy, but your personaliy makes you want to take charge and dominate others. You may come across strong and insensistive, and your sincere spiritual motivation can be misunderstood. People may accuse you of not showing mercy at all.

Choose You This Day Who and Where You Will Serve

To choose where to be involved, first pray that God will give you wisdom about how your specific personality, spiritual gifts, talents, interests and experiences relate to the needs in the church. The Lord may also direct you to get involved in ministries that don't seem to fit your giftedness. Sometimes your passions and interests create a burden to be involved in unrelated areas. God can use you in a great way as you allow Him to do His work through you.

The most practical way to discover where to serve is to consider the ministries that need your personality and spiritual gifts. For example, you may have an "S" personality with the gift of ministry/serving. Look for an opportunity to serve behind the scenes doing those things most people don't want to do, such as serving in the kitchen or library. You can receive deep satisfaction knowing God uses you to meet special needs.

If you're an "I" with the gift of exhortation, you may want to get involved in a more active and aggressive outreach opportunity. "S" types prefer more passive "friendship" evangelism or counseling.

"D"s with the gift of prophecy would serve effectively in a community awareness ministry. They prefer to perceive and declare truth.

Review all the opportunities listed with your specific personality and spiritual gift in mind. There may be other opportunities not listed. You should also consider your talents, interests, and experience. For example, you may not have an "I" personality with the gift of showing mercy, but you have a burden to win the lost. Your passion and experience will mean you fit well in an evangelism ministry.

Be sure to communicate with the appropriate ministry leader. Notify him or her about your personality type, spiritual gifts, talents, interests and experience. Ask for counsel concerning where others may think you fit best. Scripture teaches, "In the multitude of counsel there's safety," Prov. 11:14.

Temporarily volunteer to serve in various ministries. Notice how you fit and feel as you serve. Be sensitive to how the Holy Spirit uses your involvement to help others and bless you.

The following are a few suggestions where you might fit best in ministry. Remember, God may lead you to do things you don't feel qualified or comfortable doing, but God always empowers you to do what He calls you to do.

Every Christian is called to pray, witness, study the Bible, and have fellowship with other believers. Don't let any confusion over your spiritual gift or personality type discourage you from doing what the Bible commands.

"D" Types —

Carpentry	Elders	Men's Min.	Prayer	Teaching	Yard Work
Coaching	EMT	Missions	Recreation	Trustees	
Construction	Evangelism	Long Rng Pln.	Search Comm.	Ushers	
Deacons	Finances	Personnel	Security	Vehicles	
Discipleship	Media	Publicity	Steering Com.	Worship	

"I" Types —

Band	Drama	Jr. High	Photography	Summer Camp	Women's Min.
Big Brothers	Elders	Interpreting	Piano	Supper Club	Worship
Bowling	Elementary	Kid Kmp/VBS	Prayer	Support Group	Youth
Choir	Evangelism	Media	Publicity	Song Leader	Youth Choir
Coaching	Encouragemt.	Men's Min.	Receptionist	Teacher	
College/Career	Greeters	Missions	Recreation	Telephone	
Communicatn.	Graphic Arts	Music	Script. Reading.	Calling	
Concerts	High School	Newcomers	Secretary	Trustee	
Counseling	Hispanic Min.	New Mem.	Senior Adults	Usher	
Deacons	Housing	Orchestra	Single Adults	Video	
Discipleship	Visitors.	Organ	Song Leading	Visitation	

"S" Types —

Alter Counselr.	Deacons	Interpreting	Organ	Small Groups	Vehicles
Baptism	Decorating	Interc. Pray.	Physician	Sound System	Visitation
Benevolence	Discipleship	Kid Kamp/VBS	Piano	Summer	Visitors Cards
Bereaving	Elders	Kitchen	Preschool	Camp	Weddings
Big Brothers	Elementary	Library	Printing	Supper Club	Women's Min.
Book Store	Encouragemt.	Mailings	Records	Supplies	Worship
Bowling	Evangelism	Maintenance	Receptionist	Support	Writing
Carpentry	Follow-up	Meals	Refug/Hmless.	Groups	Yard Work
Children	Foods	Missions	Scripture Read.	Tape Ministry	Youth Choir
Child Care	Grounds	Newcomers	Search Com.	Teaching	
Cleaning	Hispanic Min.	New Mem.	Secretary	Telephone	
Clerical	Hospital	Newsletter	Senior Adults	Calling	
College/Career	Hospice	Nurse	Serving Meals	Tutor	
Communion	Housing	Nursery	Set-up	Transportation	
Concerts	Visitors	Office Machn.	Shut-ins	Trustees	
Counseling	Infant/Todd.	Orchestra	Single Adults	Ushers	

"C" Types —

Accounting	Deacons	Grounds	Nursery	Records	Tutor
Band	Decorating	Infants Todd.	Office	Scrip. Reader	Trustee
Benevolence	Discipleship	Interpreting	Machin.	Search Com.	Vehicles
Book Store	Drama	Kitchen	Orchestra	Secretarial	Video
Carpentry	Elders	Library	Organ	Security	Visitors Cards
Children	Electrical	Mailings	Personnel	Serving Meals	Weddings
Cleaning	EMT	Long Rng. Pln.	Photography	Set-up	Worship
Clerical	Evangelism	Maintenance	Physician	Sound System	Writing
Communion	Finances	Meals	Piano	Supplies	Yard Work
Computer	Follow-up	Missions	Prayer	Steering Com.	
Concerts	Food	Music	Preschool	Tape Ministry	
Construction	Floral Arrang	Newsletter	Printing	Teaching	
Curriculum	Graphic Arts	Nurse	Publicity	Transportation	

Opportunities For Ministry

Every Christian needs to be involved in a ministry. Service encourages spiritual growth. You can experience tremendous blessing when you minister to others.

Not only do you need to serve, the church also needs servants. Nearly every ministry lacks people who will give of themselves to help others. Believers should donate their time and talents as Stewards of God.

Both you and the church will benefit when ministry results. The following are suggestions where you may "fit" best in serving the Lord.

Prayerfully review each opportunity, keeping in mind your personality and spiritual gifts. Place an "E" next to each area in which you have experience. Place an "I" in the areas you find interesting. Try to choose 3 opportunities where you want to serve. Share the choices with your minister or a leader who can give you wise counsel. Ask them to help you find a specific place of ministry where you can exercise your gifts.

There are many other opportunities of ministry not listed. You may even want to start a new one. *Grow For It!*

1. ___ Accounting		15. ___ Cleaning
2. ___ Adult Choir		16. ___ Clerical
3. ___ Altar Counselor		17. ___ Coaching
4. ___ Band		18. ___ College / Career
5. ___ Baptism		19. ___ Communication
6. ___ Benevolence		20. ___ Communion
7. ___ Bereaving		21. ___ Computer
8. ___ Big Brothers		22. ___ Concerts
9. ___ Bookstore		23. ___ Construction
10. ___ Bowling		24. ___ Counseling
11. ___ Carpentry		25. ___ Curriculum
12. ___ Child Care		26. ___ Decorating
13. ___ Children		27. ___ Deacons
14. ___ Choir		28. ___ Discipleship

29. ___ Drama
30. ___ Elders
31. ___ Electrical
Elementary
    32. ___ Sunday
    33. ___ Mid-week
    34. ___ Special Events
35. ___ EMT
36. ___ Encouragement
37. ___ Evangelism
38. ___ Finances
39. ___ Floral Arrangements
40. ___ Follow-up
41. ___ Foods
42. ___ Graphic Arts
43. ___ Greeters
44. ___ Grounds
45. ___ Hispanic Ministry
High School
    46. ___ Sunday
    47. ___ Mid-week
    48. ___ Special Events
49. ___ Housing Visitor
50. ___ Hospitals
51. ___ Hospitality
52. ___ Hospice
Infants / Toddlers
    53. ___ Sunday
    54. ___ Mid-week
    55. ___ Special Events
56. ___ Interpreting for the Deaf
57. ___ Intercessory Prayer
Jr. High
    58. ___ Sunday
    59. ___ Mid-week
    60. ___ Special Events
61. ___ Kid's Kamp / VBS
62. ___ Kitchen

63. ___ Library
64. ___ Long Range Planning
65. ___ Mailings
66. ___ Maintenance
67. ___ Martial Arts
68. ___ Meals
69. ___ Media
70. ___ Men's Ministries
71. ___ Men's Softball
72. ___ Men's Basketball
73. ___ Missions
74. ___ Musician
75. ___ Newcomers
76. ___ New Members
77. ___ Newsletter
78. ___ Nurse
79. ___ Nursery
80. ___ Office Machines
81. ___ Orchestra
82. ___ Organ
83. ___ Personnel
84. ___ Photography
85. ___ Physician
86. ___ Piano
87. ___ Prayer
Preschool
    88. ___ Sunday
    89. ___ Mid-week
    90. ___ Special Events
91. ___ Printing
92. ___ Publicity
93. ___ Records
94. ___ Receptionist
95. ___ Recreation
96. ___ Refugee/Homeless Min.
97. ___ Scripture Reader
98. ___ Search
99. ___ Secretarial

100. ___ Security
101. ___ Senior Adults
102. ___ Serving Meals
103. ___ Set-up
104. ___ Shut-Ins
105. ___ Single Adults
106. ___ Single Parents
107. ___ Small Groups
108. ___ Song Leading
109. ___ Sound System
110. ___ Steering
111. ___ Summer Camp
112. ___ Supplies
113. ___ Supper Club
114. ___ Support Groups
115. ___ Tape Ministry
116. ___ Teaching

117. ___ Telephone Calling
118. ___ Tutoring
119. ___ Transportation
120. ___ Trustees
121. ___ Ushers
122. ___ Vehicles
123. ___ Video
124. ___ Visitation
125. ___ Visitor Cards
126. ___ Weddings
127. ___ Women's Ministries
128. ___ Women's Softball
129. ___ Worship Leader
130. ___ Writing
131. ___ Yard Work
132. ___ Youth
133. ___ Youth Choir

Fitly Joined Together

The following are opportunities for ministry in relationship to spiritual gifts. With your gifts in mind, look at all the ministries available. You should also consider many other gifts not included. You may also have various passions and interests that would cause you to fit well in a specific ministry.

If you are already involved in a ministry that doesn't seem to match, don't think you shouldn't be involved. Remember Moses!

Your past and present experiences should also enter into your search for a good fit. In summary, consider your spiritual gifts, personality type, interests, passions and experiences in making your choices. Once you have chosen 3 - 5 opportunities for ministry, be sure to notify your pastor, a spiritual leader or ministry coordinator. Then get involved as soon as possible.

Lets look at involvement from our spiritual gifts perspective.

Evangelism | Teaching | Pastor / Shepherd

Evangelism		Teaching	Pastor / Shepherd	
Altar Counsel.	Nurse	Bookstore	Altar Counsel.	Prayer
Big Brothers	Orchestra	Clerical	Baptism	Preschool
Bowling	Photography	Coaching	Big Brothers	Publicity
Carpentry	Physician	Computer	Clerical	Script. Reader
Cleaning	Prayer	Curriculum	College/Career	Search Comm.
Coaching	Printing	Deacons	Communication	Senior Adults
Communication	Publicity	Discipleship	Communion	Single Adults
Concerts	Receptionist	Elders	Counseling	Single Parents
Construction	Recreation	Electrical	Curriculum	Small Groups
Counseling	Refug/Hmless	Elementary	Deacons	Song Leader
Deacons	Senior Adults	Finances	Discipleship	Steering Comm.
Discipleship	Single Adults	Interpreting	Elders	Tape Ministry
Drama	Single Parents	Library	Elementary	Teaching
Elders	Small Groups	Men's Ministry	Encouragement	Tutoring
Electrical	Song Leader	Missions	Evangelism	Trustees
Evangelism	Steering Comm.	Prayer	Hispanic Min.	Video
Foods	Supper Club	Printing	High School	Visitation
Greeters	Tape Ministry	Records	Intercess. Pray.	Women's Min.
High School	Telephone Call.	Script. Reader	Jr. High	Worship
Housing Visit.	Tutoring	Search Comm.	Media	Writing
Jr. High	Transportation	Steering Comm.	Men's Min.	Youth
Kids Kamp/VBS	Trustees	Tape Ministry	Missions	Youth Choir
Martial Arts	Ushers	Teaching	Newsletter	
Meals	Video	Tutoring	Personnel	
Media	Visitation	Trustees		
Men's Ministry	Woman's Min.	Video		
Missions	Writing	Women's Min.		
Musician	Youth	Worship		
Newcomers	Youth Choir	Writing		
Newsletter				

Ministry / Serving

Adult Choir	Discipleship	Jr. High	Piano	Tape Ministry
Altar Counsel.	Drama	Kids Kamp/VBS	Prayer	Teaching
Band	Elders	Kitchen	Preschool	Telephone Call.
Baptism	Electrical	Library	Printing	Tutoring
Bereaving	Elementary	Mailings	Publicity	Transportation
Big Brothers	EMT	Maintenance	Records	Trustees
Bookstore	Encouragement	Martial Arts	Receptionist	Ushers
Bowling	Evangelism	Meals	Recreation	Vehicles
Carpentry	Floral Arrange.	Media	Script. Reader	Video
Child Care	Foods	Men's Ministry	Secretarial	Visitation
Children	Graphic Arts	Missions	Senior Adults	Visitors Cards
Choir	Greeters	Musician	Serving Meals	Weddings
Cleaning	Grounds	Newcomers	Set-up	Women's Min.
Clerical	Hispanic Min.	Newsletter	Shut-ins	Worship
Coaching	High School	Nurse	Single Adults	Writing
College/Career	Housing Visit.	Nursery	Single Parents	Yard Work
Communion	Hospital	Office Machines	Small Groups	Youth
Concerts	Hospitality	Orchestra	Song Leader	Youth Choir
Construction	Hospice	Organ	Sound System	
Counseling	Infants/Toddl.	Personnel	Steering Comm.	
Decorating	Interpreting	Photography	Supplies	
Deacons	Intercess. Pray.	Physician	Supper Club	

Prophecy

Coaching
Communication
Deacons
Discipleship
Elders
Evangelism
Finances
Long Ran. Plan.
Martial Arts
Media
Men's Ministry
Newsletter
Personnel
Prayer
Printing
Records
Script. Reader
Search Comm.
Security
Steering Comm.
Tape Ministry
Teaching
Trustees
Visitation
Women's Min.
Writing

Exhortation

Altar Counsel.
Adult Choir
Band
Big Brothers
Choir
Coaching
College/Career
Communication
Concerts
Counseling
Deacons
Discipleship
Drama
Elders
Encouragement
Evangelism
High School

Jr. High
Media
Men's Ministry
Newsletter
Nurse
Prayer
Printing
Receptionist
Script. Reader
Single Parents
Tape Ministry
Teaching
Trustees
Video
Visitation
Women's Min.
Worship
Writing

Mercy

Bereaving
Big Brothers
Carpentry
Child Care
Children
Cleaning
Communion
Construction
Counseling
Deacons
Discipleship
Elders
Elementary
EMT
Evangelism
Foods
Greeters
Housing Visit.
Hospital
Hospice
Infants/Toddl.
Interpreting
Intercess. Pray.
Kids Kam/VBS

Kitchen
Meals
Newcomers
Nurse
Nursery
Organ
Physician
Piano
Prayer
Preschool
Refug/Homless
Serving Meals
Set-up
Shut-ins
Telephone Call.
Tutoring
Trustees
Weddings
Women's Min.
Worship
Writing
Yard Work

Giving

Accounting
Benevolence
Bookstore
Clerical
Coaching
Computer
Construction
Curriculum
Decorating
Deacons
Discipleship
Elders
Electrical
EMT
Finances
Floral Arrange.
Foods
Graphic Arts

Grounds
Housing Visit.
Kitchen
Library
Long Ran. Plan.
Mailings
Maintenance
Meals
Media
Men's Ministry
Missions
Musician
Newcomers
Newsletter
Nursery
Office Machines
Orchestra

Administration / Ruling

Accounting
Benevolence
Clerical
Construction
Counseling
Deacons
Discipleship
Elders
Finances
Foods
Grounds
Kitchen
Library
Long Ran. Plan.
Mailings
Maintenance
Meals
Media
Men's Min.
Missions

Newsletter
Personnel
Physician
Prayer
Printing
Publicity
Records
Refug/Hmless
Search Comm.
Security
Single Parents
Sound System
Steering Com.
Supplies
Tape Ministry
Transportation
Trustees
Vehicles
Video
Women's Min.

These lists are loose and basic suggestions for where you may fit best. If your current ministry or interests are not listed under your top three spiritual gifts do not be alarmed. These lists cannot measure the will or calling of God. He sometimes calls us to do things we're not gifted to do. Moses probably would never have found "administration / ruling" as his spiritual gift, but God still used him as a great leader.

You may also have an interest or passion for a specific ministry that is not listed under your spiritual gifts. Don't let that discourage you. We could not list every conceivable ministry under each of the gifts. The most important thing to remember is that God has gifted you to be a blessing through your special motivations. Let these motivations stimulate you toward greater ministry. You will then experience the joy of the Lord like you may have never seen before.

Part 4

Conflict Resolution

16

Handling The Hot Potato Of Conflict

Most churches are crippled because of broken relationships and bruised friendships. Instead of waging war against the enemies of the faith, church members attack each other. Casualties can be seen from the Sunday School room to the choir room, from the pastor's office to the parking lot, and from the kitchen to the nursery. Unified armies of God have become fragmented pockets of resistance. Brother against brother and sister against sister, this un-civil war is the shame of the church and disgrace of grace. Churches, which possess the greatest love story ever told, have become front page news of animosity, suspicion, and division.

Conflicts are like hot potatoes. No one wants to handle them. They burn. They scar. They hurt, but someone has to deal with them. Conflicts are inevitable. In fact, the more people involved, the more potential for conflict. What baffles me is why so many churches today are not putting as much emphasis on conflict resolution as they are on networking and ministry placement.

In *The Cross of Christ*, John Stott outlines the revolutionary way believers are to treat those who offend them:

> Now Paul writes: "Bless those who persecute you" (Rom 12:14), and "if your enemy is hungry, feed him" (12:20). We are to wish good to people by blessing them, and to do good to people by serving them. In the new community of Jesus curses are to be replaced by blessings, malice by prayer, and revenge by service. In fact, prayer purges the heart of malice; the lips which bless cannot simultaneously curse; and the hand occupied with service is restrained from taking revenge.[1]

Stott continues,

> The tragedy of repaying evil for evil is that we thereby add evil to evil and so *increase* the world's tally of evil. It causes what Martin Luther King called "the chain reaction of evil", as hate multiplies hate and violence multiplies violence in "a descending spiral of destruction." The glory of loving and serving our enemies, however, is that we thereby *decrease* the amount of evil in the world. The supreme example is the cross. Christ's willingness to bear the scorn of men and the wrath of God has brought salvation to millions. The cross is the only alchemy which turns evil into good.[2]

It seems like everyone has jumped on the assimilation bandwagon. Churches frantically work on programs to get more members involved but seem to have forgotten the potentially negative relational consequences of this involvement. Please don't misunderstand me. I'm not against involving more people in ministry. In fact, I'm 100% for it. But involving people without giving them the skills to work together may create bigger problems than having people uninvolved.

Ministries should have a system for members to know about and practice biblical conflict resolution. Ironically, the world is better at conflict management than the church. It probably has something to do with the almighty dollar. Employees are bound by their pay checks to work out their problems, but pastors, staffs, and church members simply move from church to church—or move their pastor and staff members—if their differences cannot be resolved.

I'm sometimes asked by churches to mediate a conflict between pastor and staff or deacons and staff. Personnel Committees hire me to help resolve differences. I always ask if the personnel committee has an "Open Door Policy" where anyone can come to them and share anything about anyone? Their response is always a quick, "Of course, yes!"

I then seriously ask, "Do you know that's wrong?"

Their immediate response is, "But we've always done it that way."

For centuries, church leaders have not practiced church discipline and policies to divert potential or real divisions. Instead of going directly to those who have hurt them, members go to deacons, committees, staff members, and pastors to share how they have been offended by others in the church. The Bible is clear on how this practice and policy is wrong. More Christians have been destroyed by their "friends" than by any of the world's devices. The devil has often stepped back and let our own human nastiness destroy one another. We have become our worst enemies.

Whenever two or more people work, worship, or live together, there will eventually be differences of opinions. This is not to say there will always be conflicts. Clashes usually occur because people have their own ways of thinking, feeling, and acting.

Most problems in ministry are not theological or technical. They are more relational. Therefore, we must understand and practice Biblical Resolution Management. The Bible is clear concerning what we should do whenever we have a conflict with someone.

The more people involved in ministry, the more chances for conflicts exist. As maturing Christians, we must understand how group dynamics create potential conflicts. Unfortunately, many Christians avoid conflicts by avoiding involvement in ministry.

Imagine how it must have been the morning of the Day of Pentecost. It was the *"birthday"* of the Church. It was going to be one of the greatest days in the history of humankind. God was going to pour out His Spirit on all believers.

If you had volunteered to help on that day, you would have been a little excited and/or nervous, confused, and frustrated. Thousands of people were pouring into Jerusalem.

Imagine being in charge of parking. Many people must have complained, *"We don't have enough donkey spaces for everyone."*

Imagine being in charge of the sound system. The sound in the room where the disciples were praying was as of a mighty rushing wind. It was too loud. It was more than you could handle. It was out of control.

What if you were in charge of ushering? Where were you going to put all those people? Crowd control must have been difficult. What if you were in charge of interpreting? There were people from every language and nation. It was impossible to handle.

Imagine the confusion and chaos there must have been. If you were a volunteer, how would you have responded? Would it have been too much to handle? But it was the *"birthday"* of the church! God was doing a work that has never been duplicated since.

"D"s and "I"s must have loved it. "S"s and "C"s must have been frustrated. Those with the gifts of prophecy and exhortation were excited, while those with the gifts of administration / ruling, teaching, and giving must have questioned Christ.

When God does a great work, there is often confusion and

disorganization. We cannot humanly keep up with what God does miraculously. When God blesses a church in a miraculous way, there will usually never be enough workers, finances, or facilities. But that's what miracles are all about.

Imagine what it must have been like when Jesus told the disciples to feed the 5,000. Thomas must have freaked out. He no doubt thought, *"This is crazy. We only have five loaves and two fishes. Jesus has gone too far!"*

Most churches are crippled from lack of faith and vision. Too many "S"s and "C"s are not willing or ready for change. "D"s and "I"s also add to the problem by not being patient and loving enough to wait on their brothers and sisters in Christ to adapt and change.

The exciting reality is that God has not finished with us (Philippians 1:6). He continues to work —conforming us into the image of Christ (Romans 8:29).

Even though the way we feel and think has definitely been influenced by our past, it does not have to control us. Happiness is a choice. We can allow our personalities and spiritual gifts to control our flesh or we can control our giftedness for God's glory.

We must guard against selfish responses. Better yet, we can allow the Holy Spirit to master our temperaments — to temper and strengthen us for His glory. We can allow the Holy Spirit to use our spiritual gifts beyond what we ever imagined.

Nothing has stifled spiritual and numerical growth in the church more than our dissensions and divisions. The greatest hindrance to spiritual growth is conflict. Excited Christians who want to serve God are often discouraged because they see—and often experience firsthand—misunderstandings and clashes with other Christians. This chapter is designed to help you discover why people do what they do under pressure and why people have conflicts with others. Scripture is clear on how to handle clashes, but many Christians are not aware of their "sensitive spots." Believers need to learn what the Bible teaches about resolving conflicts.

Every personality has its "hot button." Everyone can act like a "D" when pushed too far. The following descriptions are tendencies of personalities when they are under pressure. Most problems in the church today are not theological—they're relational —personality conflicts and clashes with others. Notice how you respond to conflicts, then develop an action plan to be "spirit-controlled," rather than controlled by your feelings.

Often, the greatest hindrances to healthy relationships are personality conflicts. Positive individuals, desiring to build good relationships, are often discouraged because of misunderstandings and clashes with others.

The following is designed to help you discover why people do what they do under pressure and why you may conflict with others. Life's success principles on how to handle clashes are clear. The problem is many people are not aware of their *"sensitive spots."* Everyone needs to learn more about avoiding and resolving conflicts.

Every personality has its *"hot button."* Everyone can act like a "D" when pushed too far. The following are tendencies of personalities as they relate under pressure.

Review the following pages with your Behavioral Blends in mind. Read each section to see how you may respond as a specific personality type. Also consider how you may respond differently because of your "hot and cold buttons."

To improve your effectiveness, control your personality and spiritual gifts. Never use them as excuses for poor behavior!

Most problems today are not technical—
they're relational —
personality conflicts and clashes with others.

How Specific Personality Types Respond To Conflict

Under pressure "D"s become dictatorial, domineering, demanding, angry, intense, forceful, direct, and bossy.

Their sources of irritation are weakness, indecisiveness, laziness, **and the lack of** discipline, planning, purpose, direction, authority, control, and challenge.

"D"s need to back off, seek peace, relax, think before reacting, control their responses, and be patient, loving, friendly, loyal, kind, and sensitive.

Under pressure "I"s become hyper, overly optimistic, immature, emotional, irrational, silly, wordy, and selfish.

Their sources of irritation are disinterest, slowness, pessimism, details, time restraints, antagonism, doubt, structure, **and the lack of** enthusiasm and team participation.

"I"s need to listen, count the cost, control their emotions, and be humble, strong, disciplined, punctual, careful with words, and conscientious.

Under pressure "S" behavior becomes subservient, insecure, fearful, weak willed, and withdrawn. This person sympathizes too much and may be naive.

Their sources of irritation are pushiness, instability, inflexibility, anger, disloyalty, insensitivity, pride, discrimination, and unfairness.

"S"s need to be strong, courageous, challenging, aggressive, assertive, confrontational, enthusiastic, outgoing, expressive, cautious, and bold.

Under pressure "C"s become moody, critical, contemplative, negative, and worrisome.

Their sources of irritation are incompetence, disorganization, foolishness, dishonesty, inaccuracy, wastefulness, inconsistency, blind faith, and false impressions.

"C"s need to loosen up, communicate, and be joyful, positive, tolerant, compromising, open, trusting, and enthusiastic.

Natural and Recommended Responses

Natural Responses To Conflict —

"D"s—attack

"I"s—expose others

"S"s—support or submit

"C"s—criticize

Recommended Biblical Responses —

"D"s—restore with love

"I"s—talk To God, not others

"S"s—care enough to confront

"C"s—examine yourself first

Practical Application

To see how our differences affect us, consider two people with different personalities serving on the benevolence committee. One person has a high "D"; the other person has a high "S." The "D" characteristically believes, "If you don't work, you don't eat." The "S" is merciful and feels everyone deserves a break. Wherever the committee has to consider the needs of members who can't pay their bills because of unemployment, sparks fly. Both committee members may be committed Christians who sincerely desire God's will. One looks at the problem as a question of dollars and responsibility. The other, however, sees the human suffering and is sensitive and caring. The "D" tends to be too hard, and the "S" tends to be too soft.

These committee members often conflict because they observe the problem from different angles. To work in harmony, they need to see the situation from the other's side. One needs to be more kind and tolerant, and the other needs to learn to be firm. They both need to be balanced.

Paul and Barnabas are good examples of Christians who disagreed. Paul had a problem with John Mark. Barnabas wanted John Mark to assist them in their journey, but Paul refused because John Mark had previously disappointed him. Acts 15:39 describes the contention between Paul and Barnabas as "so sharp between them, that they departed from each other." Paul chose Silas; Barnabas took John Mark. The division was over John Mark's involvement in the ministry, but Paul had an offense against him. Paul was obviously intolerant of John Mark's defection during a previous journey. Scripture does not suggest that John Mark had done anything wrong, but Paul was a determined man. Perhaps John Mark couldn't take Paul's powerful and authoritative personality, and he simply wanted to get away from Paul's dominance.

On the other hand, Barnabas' name means "Son of Encouragement." He was loving and kind. He was also John Mark's cousin, and "S"s are very loyal to their families. Barnabas may have been sticking up for his cousin, and he may have felt compassion for John Mark as he saw him struggle with Paul's powerful personality.

Acts 15:40 states that the brethren "recommended" them both. The leaders recognized neither was right or wrong. They simply encouraged them both. Many conflicts are neither right nor wrong; they are personality conflicts. God sometimes allows these conflicts to force us to go in separate directions. Some churches never grow until they split and try to prove their "rightness." This is obviously the wrong motivation, but God sometimes takes a crooked stick to point a straight path.

God is in the process of molding and making us into the image of Christ. This process involves heat and pressure. As "iron sharpens iron" (Prov. 27:17), God allows friction to come into our lives to sharpen our effectiveness for Christ. To sharpen iron, you place it along side a sharpening rod. You don't slam it against the rod. That will only make it blunt. You must bring it along side the rod, just touching its edge. Sparks fly and the iron is sharpened. So it is in the church. Sharpening Christians requires people to get close to each other. The closer they get, the greater the potential for sparks. Once sparks fly, it can result in sharpening our likeness of Christ. We don't want to collide with people and damage them. We simply rub against them emotionally and intellectually. We can expect friction, but we also know that God can turn sparks into spirituality, hurt into help, and pain into gain so that Christ is glorified.

ENDNOTES

[1]Stott, John R. W., *The Cross of Christ*, (Downers Grove, IL: InterVarsity Press, 1986), p. 12.

[2]Ibid., p. 301.

17

Biblical Resolution Management

This chapter contains a Biblical Resolution Management Covenant designed to help church members deal with conflict. No church is perfect. Conflicts happen and clear policies must be in place to take members step-by-step through the process of restoration and healing.

The most important question is, "Do we want to expose our offending brother or do we want to restore him?" Most conflicts are mismanaged because people want to analyze and discuss all the faults of others. For God to be glorified in all we say and do, we must seek the higher road of seeing the beam in our eye and desire others' good above our own. To solve our problems with others, Christ's glory and will must be elevated above all else.

The following is a Biblical Resolution Management Covenant to help church members avoid and resolve conflicts. Every church should use this to improve their *people* problems. Churches are very weak in this area. Business and industry are better at resolving problems than churches are. Yet churches have the best

"Manual" (the Bible) to teach them how to deal with their differences.

Read through this covenant and ask God to help you clearly understand each step. Then commit to God that you will follow this covenant.

Covenant —

In obedience to God's Holy Word and commitment to practicing Biblical Resolution Management, I promise to follow the Principle of Priorities. That is, my priorities are to glorify God, build harmony in the church, and avoid conflict. I will do as Matthew 18 admonishes—go to an offending brother "first alone."

First Step —

I will not first share the offense with another person. I am committed to restoring the relationship, rather than exposing possible sin. I recognize most problems with people are personality clashes, and I will try to understand their actions based upon their perspective.

Second Step —

If going to a person "first alone" does not resolve our differences, I promise to seek a neutral and mature individual who will listen to each of our perspectives of the problem. This person will hopefully be able to shed light on one or both of our blind spots or areas of needed growth in order to glorify God.

I recognize that the "witness" may reveal or say things I won't like, but I will believe God is using him or her to resolve the conflict, rather than take sides. (The "witness" must be an individual with deep spiritual wisdom and highly respected by all those involved.)

Warning —

I will not seek to find others who have also been offended, nor share my concerns with potential "witnesses" prior to the meeting with my "offending brother." The purpose of having a "witness" is not to validate my hurt but rather to open my heart and mind to the possible needs I may have regarding my relationship with others.

I realize my friends may naturally listen to my concerns, but also take up my offense. I will, therefore, not cause them to become a party to a possible division and disharmony because of our friendship. Whenever I feel an urge to share the offense with my friends, I will pray and commune with God about my hurt.

Confronting Ministry Leaders —

I believe in the scriptural admonition to not rebuke an Elder (spiritual leader), other than in grave matters of misconduct and open sin (1 Timothy 5:19). I will earnestly pray for and follow those God has placed in leadership over me. I will not allow anyone to criticize them without following the principles in Matthew 18 and without the specific person present.

If I have a problem with my ministry leader, I will go "first alone" to them. I will not share my concern with anyone. I will listen and try to understand their perspective of the problem. If I am not satisfied with their explanation and continue to have animosity, I will ask their permission and counsel to find a "witness" who will listen to our conflict.

If the "witness" finds I have misunderstood the situation and should continue no further, I will trust God to complete His work in my life by casting my burden on the Lord and leaving it there. If the "witness" agrees with my concern and finds the ministry leader wrong and the leader refuses to hear the "witness," we will then find a group of two or three other "witnesses" who will hear the matter and determine what God is doing through this conflict.

Serious Step —

If I continue to find fault with a ministry leader and cannot worship in "spirit and truth," I will seek to join another ministry rather than cause any conflict and disharmony. I am committed to pleasing God through resolving my conflicts, even if it means separating myself from the source of my irritations.

Ultimate Goal —

I commit myself to be spiritual rather than "normal" and supernatural rather than "natural" when it comes to solving my problems with others. I want God's will and way to resolve my conflicts and will do as the Holy Bible teaches, regardless of my normal and natural feelings.

My ultimate goal is to glorify God through bearing much fruit, getting involved in ministry, and avoiding and resolving conflicts.

A Word of Explanation

Most people believe the "witnesses" in Matthew 18:16 are people who actually witnessed the offense. There are many cases, however, when there are no actual witnesses. In other cases, bringing a group who all have offenses creates extremely defensive reactions and makes it difficult to "restore" the person. I prefer to think of the "witness" as an arbiter or mediator. This person can listen objectively. When both parties agree to have a mature brother or sister in Christ mediate or arbitrate a dispute, the probability of resolution increases dramatically.

Sometimes the problem is made worse by trying to find people who will back us, but this only adds fuel to the flames because our friends usually take up our offenses and defend us instead of being totally objective. When we tell our friends about a brother's offense, they may not have even known about the incident or problem. In this case, we have planted a seed of doubt in their minds about this person, and we have offended our offending brother.

Not long ago, a church leader told his pastor that he had seen a deacon at a pornography shop in town. The leader had noticed the deacon's car in the parking lot, so he parked across the street and waited to see if he was truly inside. After a while the deacon came out of the store, confirming the leader's disappointment. Hearing the story, the pastor interrupted and said, "Don't tell me who it is. I want you to go to him first alone." The leader went to his offending brother and expressed his concern.

The very first thing the deacon said was, "Have you told anyone?" Because the pastor really didn't know who it was, he could honestly say, "No." The exposed deacon began to cry, and he expressed how sorry he was. He admitted he needed help for his immorality.

A Tremendous Lesson

There's a tremendous lesson in this story. If the offended leader had told anyone about his weaker brother, they could have gotten into a big fight over their friendship. The stronger leader could have been confronted about telling others. People are naturally defensive when caught in a fault. If the stronger brother had not gone to the weaker brother first alone, the one who really needed help would have said, "You did wrong by not coming to me first. I did wrong and you did wrong. We're even. Now let's forget it."

That's exactly what happens subconsciously, if not openly, in churches every week. We need to practice biblical resolution management to restore our offending brothers and sisters. The most important element in avoiding and resolving conflicts is always to have the offending person present. It is amazing how stories change when the person being talked about is present.

Justice For All

Our American judicial system was influenced by biblical principles including the right to a speedy trial, the right to an attorney, the right to face our accusers, and the right to cross examine. Our courts are designed to help us deal with conflicts, and our rights are protected by law. However, the laws protect people more effectively at work than at church. Every Sunday thousands of pastors and staff members are fired, deacons dismissed, and church leaders destroyed because of unbiblical practices performed in the name of "doing God's will."

I know of a pastor who went to his regular monthly elder's meeting without any hint of a problem. He was asked for his resignation or he would be fired. He asked, "What did I do wrong?" And the chairman said, "It's over. There will be no discussion. We've already talked it over and decided to ask for your resignation." To this day, the pastor still does not know what he did to provoke his ouster. These things ought not to be!

In the business world, there has to be a reason for firing someone. There must be an explanation, especially in the church, if for no other reason than to help the pastor. It is cold-blooded assassination of his character to do otherwise. To think that so-called godly men had been meeting (probably for months) to discuss and plan the pastor's dismissal, to discuss his future without his right to a fair trial, to face his accusers, to cross examine, or to defend himself is unethical as well as unbiblical.

Most churches have very unclear ethical guidelines. Friendships, families, and finances are sometimes valued more highly than fairness. Careers are ruined, reputations smeared, and lives crushed by the weight of "so-called" evidence without thorough, objective examination of the facts.

Need For Witness

Recently in Atlanta, I heard of a murder where the key witness died of a heart attack before the trial. The FBI had to drop the case because the judge would not allow a videotaped testimony against the accused murderer. The witness was credible, and it was an "open and shut case." When the witness died, however, the defendant lost his right to cross examine. The case was thrown out of court, and the accused murderer walked free.

Our American judicial system is the best in the world. It can fail, but at least the accused are protected. In the church today, however, the accused are paraded through telephone lines, meeting rooms, and parking lots never knowing their accusers and never able to answer the questions raised. Talk about a travesty of justice in the most sacred of halls! What a contradiction! Pastors, staff, deacons, elders, trustees and lay leaders ought to say, "Enough is enough!" The church is never going to be the refuge and powerhouse God meant it to be until fairness and common decency prevail. Every church leader needs to be committed to fairness, and they should not listen to anything derogatory against their brothers and sisters in Christ without the accused present.

Every church needs to establish Biblical Resolution Management policies and procedures. New members should be informed and oriented to the church's covenant. Also, new members who bring unresolved conflicts with them should be encouraged to deal with their bitterness. Otherwise, these conflicts will surface and cause divisions again.

Past Hurts

Many people join churches because of problems in their former churches. The "Hide and Heal Syndrome" describes people who slip quietly into new churches because of past problems. These wounded saints don't want to get deeply involved again. They just want to worship and heal their hurts. They may have been some of the best deacons or Sunday school teachers, but now they simply fill the pew, sing the hymns, and smile. No one knows their hurts as they hide and heal. If churches practiced Biblical Resolution Management, these former faithful servants would feel more comfortable and able to come out of their closets. If their new church followed biblical policies and procedures to avoid and resolve conflicts, they may feel more willing to get involved again.

People, like Pavlov's dogs, will be slapped and slandered only so much until they react and retract. They will respond positively again when they know their involvement will not lead to further injury. Churches need to teach and practice Matthew 18 and 1 Timothy 5. For the church to become a mighty army, we've got to change our tune. Most churches are singing the sad song of disharmony in the minor key. The great hymns of the faith are losing their influence. Instead of "like a mighty fortress is the church of God," we could more aptly sing:

"Like a mighty tortoise moves the church of God. Brothers, we are treading where we've always trod.

Like a murky river moves the church of God, sisters we are fighting were we've always fought."

Shame on us! Let's be about the Father's business of reaching the lost and maturing the saints. Let's stop burying our wounded, and let's start healing our hurting. There's so much at stake. For Christ's sake, let's love one another.

We also need to learn how to deal with conflicts in our homes. The following chapter deals with our most intimate relationships. This information can be either convicting or confirming. These issues of resolving conflicts in our churches and families are very important. Please consider how you can apply these principles in these two vital environments. If we do, the community of believers and our families will become powerful, nurturing, life-changing places.

God Hates Discord

Remember, God hates discord. Sadly, so many churches are crippled because of disharmony. Churches would be stronger and much more effective, if they would determine to abide by Biblical Resolution Management principles. Once you get involved in ministry, conflicts are inevitable. The Bible is our perfect *"personnel manual."* It teaches us how to avoid and resolve conflicts. We must constantly remember our ultimate goal when conflicting with others — to glorify God!

We must also desire to restore our offending brothers and sisters, rather than exposing them. Keep in mind that our battle armor only covers our fronts (Helmet of Salvation, Sword of the Lord, Breastplate of Righteousness). There is nothing to protect our backs. So many Christians are wounded and become casualties, because the arrows of our fellow soldiers, behind us, fall short of their intended targets.

Little Red Riding Hood

Several years ago I read a crazy, but humorous fairy tale. This is how I remember it.

"Once upon a time, to protect herself from the big bad wolf, Little Red Riding Hood disguised herself as a wolf.

The wolf in order to sneak up on Little Red Riding Hood disguised itself as the grandmother.

And the grandmother, in order to confuse the wolf, disguised herself as Little Red Riding Hood.

The wolf, disguised as the grandmother, was able to get close enough to kill the grandmother, who was disguised as Little Red Riding Hood.

Realizing that Little Red Riding Hood was actually the grandmother, the wolf was confused. The wolf, who was disguised as the grandmother, then took off running through the woods.

Little Red Riding Hood, who was disguised as the wolf saw what happened and realized her grandmother was actually the wolf, who began running through the woods.

Little Red Riding Hood, disguised as the wolf, took off after the wolf, who was disguised as the grandmother.

Hunters, seeing a wolf, who was really Little Red Riding Hood, chasing a grandmother, who really was the big bad wolf, shot and killed Little Red Riding Hood, because they thought she was the wolf.

The wolf, disguised as the grandmother, continued running through the woods.

Other wolves, thinking the big bad wolf was a grandmother lost in the woods, attacked and killed what they thought was a grandmother, but who was really the wolf."

The moral of this story is *life can be tragic if we don't seek to know who others really are.*

18

Are You Enduring Or Enjoying Your Relationships?

When I first got married, I heard you should never go to sleep at night if you were angry with your mate. Needless to say, I didn't get much sleep the first ten years of my marriage! Conflicts are perhaps most evident in the home. "Home Sweet Home" has become the battlefield of daily living, and "Feuding Families" are commonplace.

Strained relationships result when we don't understand each other. The closer our relationships, the more vulnerable we become. That's why conflicts in trusted, intimate relationships hurt the most. With personality differences in mind, looking at our relationships can be enlightening. As previously mentioned, opposites both attract and attack. To survive the relationship "rat trap," we need to understand the dynamic differences at work in our relationships.

Understanding the contrasts in personalities is not only enlightening, it is practical. Each person must learn to give and take. When only one person is giving or taking, the relationship eventually will be challenged. Roles in relationships are confusing and diverse, especially in our culture. Who's the boss? Why does any-one have to be the boss? This subject is perhaps the most volatile of all when it comes to marriage and relationships.

Chain of Command

Before the Fall, man and woman were equal partners. One of the results of the Fall is that there is now a chain of command in marriage. The husband is to be the head of the home. Just as a business, army, or organization involving more than one person needs a structure of authority, so does the home. God designated man to be the loving leader. But in a Christian relationship where husband and wife are both committed to the Lord Jesus Christ as Head, both the man and woman are of equal value. The role of the husband as the head of the family is not a value statement, only a delineation of roles.

Scripture is clear concerning the practical aspects of submit-ting ourselves one to the other (Eph. 5:21) and making relationships work. Husbands are wise to submit to their wives at times and in areas where their wives are stronger. I know women who can ne-gotiate the purchase of a new car better than their husbands. In this case, it would be financially and emotionally better for the wife to take charge and make the final decision. This doesn't mean the husband is not to be the spiritual leader of the home. Like a new second lieutenant in Vietnam who allowed the experienced sergeant to decide what was best, the personality wise husband knows his weaknesses and his wife's strengths. Every harmonious and suc-cessful relationship is built on an understanding of each other's tem-peraments.

Genesis 2:18 tells us God made woman to be a "help meet" for her husband. Unfortunately, some men believe this means "slave," but Scripture clearly teaches that God created woman because man needed her. The word "help meet" literally means she is "fit" for him. God gave Eve to Adam to complete him. (You may sometimes think God gave your wife to you to finish you off!)

The great philosopher, Rocky Balboa, perhaps said it best: "Adriane's got gaps and I've got gaps, but together we got no gaps." (By the way, most people don't realize "Adriane" is Mrs. Balboa's middle name. Her first name is Yo!) Like two forks meshing together and filling in the gaps, so Adam and Eve became one.

Our differences draw us together. Ironically, those same differences can drive us apart. The characteristics of the person with whom we fell in love often become the very traits we resent.

Submitted To Each Other

This idea taught me there are times when I should submit my will to my wife's will, if we are to make our marriage work. She has strengths that compensate for my weaknesses and vice versa. We complement each other, and that's how it's supposed to work. We need each other to function as a cohesive team.

The disciples Peter and Andrew were brothers who were opposites. It was Andrew who first answered Jesus' call to become a "fisher of men." Andrew then introduced Peter to the Lord. From that point, Peter became the leader. He out-shined and out-talked his brother on every occasion. Peter became the self-appointed speaker for the disciples. Andrew, on the other hand, was only seen three more times in the New Testament. Each time, Andrew is found behind the scenes.

Peter was outgoing and active; Andrew was reserved and quiet. One wasn't better than the other. Both were chosen by Christ to be disciples. In fact, if it hadn't been for Andrew's active, optimistic behavior, Peter may not have been reached with the news about Christ. Andrew may have been more comfortable behind the scenes in view of his personality, but in the Spirit, he became outgoing and assertive. He didn't hold back in telling his brother about Christ.

Though Peter and Andrew were opposites, they worked together for God's glory.

Opposites Attract and Attack

Opposites attract each other. Somehow we are attracted to people who have strengths that are our weaknesses. "C"s meet an exciting, positive, upbeat type person like an "I" and wish they were more like him or her. "I"s areimpressed with "C"s' logical thinking and organized behavior.

While opposites often attract, we must keep in mind that most people are blends or composites of DISC. Few people are predominantly "D," "I," "S," or "C." Most people are a combination of these types.

Let's review—"D/I"s are active in their tasks and people skills. "S/C"s are passive, but both people and task-oriented. "D/C"s are purely task-oriented but may be active or passive in given situations. "I/S"s are basically people-oriented and can be either active or passive.

The "I/C" can be either active or passive as well as people-and task-oriented at the same time. The same goes for the "D/S." The "I/C" loves to inspire and correct, but the "D/S" enjoys dominating and serving others. The "D/S" type may sound like a contradiction in terms, but this unique and often confusing behavior is normal for these people.

The most obvious conflicts occur when a "D/C" task-oriented individual is attracted to an "I/S" people-oriented person. These people may have been initially impressed with the others' strengths which were their own weaknesses. The "D/C" lacks people skills; the "I/S" needs to become more task-oriented and organized. The exciting news is that each needs the other, but difficulty comes when one stops looking at the strengths and focuses on the weaknesses. The "D/C" focuses on logical thinking and being industrious, while the "I/S" desires to build relationships and deepen communication. You can see how these two blends of behavior can clash.

People often wonder, "What is the perfect personality?" or "Who has the best blend of DISC?" God made us unique. We differ from one another, but God created everyone in His image. There is no "best" personality, and God didn't give anyone a "bad temperament." The perfect personality is the one controlled by the Holy Spirit. Regardless of our natural drives and motivations, the ideal blend of DISC is the one that God gave each of us individually.

Jesus was a perfect blend of all the strengths. We see Him in the temple as a "D" whipping out the money changers. He was an "I" inspiring the crowds that came to hear Him. As an "S," He said, "Don't hinder the little children to come to me." And as a "C," He expounded the deep truths of God.

Contrasting Two Personalities

The following paragraphs depict how two specific personality types relate in work and social environments.

"D" / "D" RELATIONSHIP

Work Index: Two "D"s can work well together as long as one recognizes the other is the boss. "D" #1 may be the boss, but "D" # 2 must respect and trust him.

Social Index: Two "D"s living together will struggle over who's the boss. They must learn to give and take. "D" # 2 may be a little more dominant, but "D" # 1 is also very dominant.

Practical Application

- Take turns making major decisions.
- Choose who will decide in specific areas.
- Don't give ultimatums.
- Don't force issues.
- Slow down in making decisions.

- Control yourself, rather than the other.
- Learn to relax and control stress.

"D" / "I" RELATIONSHIP

Work Index: "D"s and "I"s working together are very active. The "D" wants to control, while the "I" wants to impress. The "I" wants to talk, while the "D" works.

Social Index: The "D" tends to dominate, while the "I" desires to communicate. The "I" feels as though the "D" doesn't care, and the "D" thinks the "I" is too sensitive. "D"s are too serious; "I"s are too impulsive.

Practical Application
- Determine to communicate on the basis of the other person's needs.
- "D"s need to show they really care.
- "I"s need to give "D"s a chance to talk.
- "D"s should praise "I"s more.
- "I"s should be more industrious.
- Don't intimidate or manipulate.

"D" / "S" RELATIONSHIP

Work Index: "D"s and "S"s working together are like masters and slaves. "D"s tell "S"s what to do. "D"s need to appreciate "S"s for their hard work.

Social Index: "D"s definitely dominate "S"s, but should never take them for granted. "S"s feel secure with "D"s as long as "D"s show controlled and stable behavior. "S"s should be assertive; "D"s more compromising.

Practical Application
- "D"s should not dominate "S"s. "Submit yourself one to the other."
- Agree that when the "D" is out of control, the "S" has the

right to say so without fear.
- "S"s need to speak assertively when "D"s behavior is unacceptable.
- "S"s should show more determination.

"D" / "C" RELATIONSHIP

Work Index: A "D" and "C" working together conflict over dreams and details. The "D" wants to get the job done, and the "C" wants to get it done right.

Social Index: "D"s and "C"s are both task-oriented. "D"s are optimistic while "C"s are more pessimistic or ("realistic" to the "C"). "D"s need to be more careful; "C"s need to be more positive.

Practical Application
- Be more understanding of the other's perspectives. Don't criticize his personality.
- Allow others to feel the way they feel.
- "D"s ought to listen more to "C"s.
- "C"s should avoid the tendency to be negative.
- Give "C"s a chance to think about decisions.
- "C"s should take some risks; "D"s should be more careful.

"I" / "I" RELATIONSHIP

Work Index: Two "I"s working together will talk more than work. They compete for praise and approval. They tend to be overly optimistic and enthusiastic.

Social Index: Two "I"s working or living together will communicate well, if one doesn't out-talk the other. Both want attention and both tend to be emotional. Communication goes two ways: talking and listening.

Practical Application
- Take turns talking.
- Ask the other to repeat what he or she heard. "I"s don't

listen well.
- Record what you agreed upon so there will be no misunderstandings.
- Praise each other more than seeking to be praised.

"I" / "S" RELATIONSHIP

Work Index: "I"s and "S"s don't tend to be very industrious. They like to "care and share." "I"s are great at public relations, and "S"s tend to enjoy customer service.

Social Index: "I"s and "S" relate well together. "I"s are talkers, and "S"s are listeners. "I"s want "S"s to tell them how they feel, but "S"s can't seem to get a word in. "I"s love crowds; "S"s prefer small groups.

Practical Application
- When an "I" asks an "S" a question, the "I" should wait for the "S" to answer.
- "S"s shouldn't let "I"s interrupt and control conversations.
- "S"s should ask "I"s to repeat what "S"s say. "I"s tend to think of what they want to say next, rather than listen.

"I" / "C" RELATIONSHIP

Work Index: "I"s and "C"s make good associates when the "I"s do the selling and "C"s do the paper work. "I"s dislike "C"s pessimism, and "C"s distrust "I"s global and enthusiastic interpretation of facts.

Social Index: Due to their differences, "I"s and "C"s often conflict. "I"s are active and "C"s are passive. "I"s are feeling-oriented; "C"s are task-oriented. They are opposites, but they can complement each other.

Practical Application
- "I"s need to trust "C"s' concerns.
- "C"s ought to be more optimistic about "I"s' interests.

- "I"s should do their homework before trying to convince "C"s about an idea.
- "C"s need to express themselves instead of internally criticizing "I"s.

"S" / "S" RELATIONSHIP

Work Index: Two "S"s work best together. They don't compete or criticize each other, and they are loyal and sensitive to the other. They make great associates.

Social Index: "S"s are the most tolerant and forgiving people, therefore they make the best of friends. They aren't assertive, and they often struggle with decision-making. They can be taken advantage of if they are not careful.

Practical Application

- "S"s should force themselves to express their feelings.
- Two "S"s can miss great opportunities because neither one wants to take risks.
- Try not to depend on the other for major decisions.
- Be more enthusiastic and outgoing.

"S" / "C" RELATIONSHIP

Work Index: "S"s and "C"s working together will be passive and methodical. Precision and propriety come before performance. "S"s want "C"s to be more friendly.

Social Index: "C"s can be too picky, but "S"s will be forgiving. "S"s desire more intimacy while "C"s can be consumed by their projects. They are both more quiet and private. They can coexist with little conversation.

Practical Application

- "S"s need to pursue more depth of conversation with "C"s.
- Work together on projects.
- "C"s should not criticize "S"s' disinterest.

- Be more intimate and aggressive.
- Don't wait on others to express themselves.
- Be more optimistic and positive about your problems.

"C" / "C" RELATIONSHIP

Work Index: Two "C"s working together can be challenging. Both have high standards on how to do things. "C"s tend to think their way is best.

Social Index: Two "C"s living together often will debate about "right and wrong." They can be cold and caustic. "C"s tend to be picky perfectionists who demand competence. They make a great team when they are at peace.

Practical Application

- Be more complimentary of each other.
- Don't criticize each other's work.
- Don't keep your feelings in.
- Be more expressive and positive.
- Think twice before saying what you think.
- Compromise your way of doing things.
- Be more outgoing and people-oriented.

Dating Insights

Every personality type has its predictable pattern of behavior. Dating allows you the opportunity to get to know the other person, but it can be one of the most deceitful times of a relationship! Everyone has "masked" and "unmasked" behavior or "guarded" and "unguarded" behavior. Our "masked" or "guarded" behavior is what we think others expect of us. It's the way we perceive others expect us to act. It is our response to our environment.

"Unmasked" and "unguarded" behavior is the "real you." It's the way we really feel, our instinctive response, and basic style. Most people exhibit some blend of both "masked" and "unmasked" behavior, but this can be confusing. Sometimes you won't know what is true and genuine. In dating relationships, you might think a person is naturally gentle, when in reality, he or she is potentially explosive.

Reading Personalities

A "D" can have masked "S" behavior. He may act calm and kind while inside he is ready to burst! Pressure and familiarity often bring out the best and worst in us. Observe people as they respond to pressure and stress. The real personality often comes out in unguarded situations. Also, the closer we get to someone, the more we let our guard down. The key to successful relationships is understanding and learning how to adapt to the other person's feelings, thoughts and actions.

What To Expect

The following paragraphs describe how specific personality types respond in dating situations:

- "D" types tend to be demanding and decisive in relationships. They like to dominate and determine what to do and where to go. They can be too bossy, but they are also confident and aggressive, often succeeding where others fail. "D"s make great leaders, but under pressure, they can become unbending and oppressively forceful. They must remember to be more gentle and kind when things don't go their way.
- "I"s are inspiring and influencing types of people. They talk easily and express their feelings. Emotional and enthusiastic, they are full of fun and spontaneity. They often say silly things, but they can usually talk their way out of any problem. "I"s need to listen better. They love attention, but they should learn how to share the limelight. They must always remember that others have feelings, too. "I"s are friendly and popular.

- "S"s prefer steady and stable environments. They don't like surprises. They are loyal friends. Others often take advantage of them because "S"s seem to go along with whatever others want. They need to be more assertive and expressive. Normally gentle and kind, they must practice "tough love," that is, being lovingly strong with difficult people. "S"s should also be more decisive and demanding.
- "C"s are cautious and calculating. They seem to be moody because they are quiet and contemplative. They don't like to make quick decisions, and they prefer to investigate the options before deciding. "C"s tend to be opinionated, but they are often insightful. They can become too pessimistic and miss out on exciting opportunities. "C"s need to "let their hair down" and enjoy life rather than just endure it.

Try to discern the other person's "masked" and "unmasked" behavior by identifying and understanding others' personality profiles. You will be more likely to relate to others with integrity instead of playing games and hiding behind masks.

Good communication is both art and science. In their book, *The Language of Love*, Gary Smalley and John Trent encourage us to develop our skills of communicating by using vivid word pictures:

> . . . an emotional word picture creates a mist in your listener's mind. It forces him to strain mentally to see what lies beyond your story. And when the fog lifts, the person finally breaks out into a more clear understanding of what you wanted to express.[1]

Author's Note

Many resources are now available to help us understand people. This book may have helped you know your temperament, and you may also want to identify the personalities of others, such as your mate, parent, teacher, employee, employer, or manager. Using the *Uniquely You Profiles,* you can identify people's predictable behavioral patterns.

You may want to give a copy of this book to friends, co-workers, or family members. Or perhaps you will want to order specific assessments which are listed in the Appendix 3. I encourage you to examine these resources and determine to use them to understand yourself and others better. Remember, this information is for relatively stable people. It is not designed to help someone who needs professional care.

I regularly conduct training seminars in churches, schools, and organizations interested in using this information to improve their effectiveness. I also use these seminars to mentor individuals who desire to become "Certified Human Behavior Consultants." Other seminar options appear in the appendix.

One of the best resources available is the *Discover Your Giftedness 3 Lessons Study Guide.* This new student's guide is designed for Christians to discover their personality type, spiritual gifts, talents, and interests. It features the first-of-its-kind explanation of how spiritual gifts and personalities relate to each other and ministry. The *DYG Guide* encourages people to practice Biblical Resolution Management and get involved in ministry. This information has helped thousands of people improve their spiritual lives. These resources benefit your understanding of yourself and others.

The following Appendices deal specifically with some hard to handle issues. Study them prayerfully with an open heart and mind. Above all, allow the Holy Spirit to teach and control you for God's glory. Remember, it's not what you know, but Who you know.

ENDNOTES
[1]Smalley, Gary, and Trent, John, *The Language of Love,* (Pomona, CA: Focus on the Family Publishing, 1988), pp. 24-25.

19

Call For Commitment

Discovering your giftedness is fascinating, but the main thing is to keep the main thing the main thing! What is the main thing? It is to *"glorify God with your body and spirit,"* 1 Cor. 6:19,20.

Scripture also admonishes us to *"present our bodies, living sacrifices to God . . . to discover what is that good and acceptable will of God,"* Rom. 12:1,2. If you really want to discover God's will for your life, you must give God your giftedness. Give Him your feelings, thoughts, and actions, both naturally with your personality and supernaturally with your spiritual gifts.

The Bible teaches to not be like children tossed to and fro, all mixed up in life. Instead we should *"speak the truth in love that we may grow up in Christ,"* Eph. 4:15. We need to mature in Christ so that we can enjoy life as God intended.

Maturing in Christ involves being *"fitly joined together"* in ministry, Eph. 4:16. Your church is the best place for you to use this tremendous learning experience. Everything would be wasted if you read this book without determining to be involved in a specific ministry; and if you didn't learn how to avoid and resolve conflicts based upon Biblical Resolution Management principles.

Consider making a commitment to follow Christ. Dedicate your giftedness to God. He wants to bless you more than you could ever imagine. Remember, happiness is a choice You will experience true joy, *"charis,"* when you are exercising your giftedness. But you must make the commitment.

Don't wait for anyone to ask you to get involved. Start this week by just showing up and saying, *"I'm ready to serve!"* Don't be surprised if things are a little disorganized and chaotic at times. Remember the Day of Pentecost!

This *Call For Commitment* could be your Day of Pentecost, when God pours out His Spirit on your life and uses you in ways you never dreamed. But it could also be a nightmare, because of *people.* Keep your eyes on Christ and you will succeed.

Success or Failure

Success in the Christian life comes as you obey and yield to the Holy Spirit's control. Allow Him to be the Lord of your emotions, will, and thoughts. God can control your personality better than you can.

Christ wants to live His life through you. Actually, you can't live the Christian life apart from Christ. Only Christ can live the Christian life in you. You must allow Him to be the Lord of your life. *"I am crucified with Christ, nevertheless I live, yet not I, but Christ lives in me. And the life that I now live in the flesh, I live by the faith of the Son of God who loved me and gave Himself for me,"* Gal. 2:20.

You CAN live the Christian life through Christ. *"I can do all things through Christ who strengthens me,"* Phil. 4:13. The difference between this truth and humanism is the humanist starts with *"I"* and ends with *"things."* The Bible and Human Behavior Science from a biblical perspective begins with God — *"In the beginning God created"* and ends with Christ — *"I can do all things through Christ."*

Be all that you can be. You can do all things through Christ. But *"whatsoever you do, do it heartily as unto Christ and not unto men,"* Col. 3:23. And *"whatsoever things you do, do all to the glory of God,"* 1 Cor. 10:31.

Hopefully you now have a better idea of where you fit best in ministry. The information you have learned should help you understand yourself and others better. But don't stop here. Go on to maturity, involvement, and more harmonious ministry.

Be sure to get with your Pastor or Involvement Coordinator and find your special ministry in the church. Get involved ASAP. Also make a commitment to Biblical Resolution Management.

Above all, allow God to use your giftedness for His glory.

Appendices

Appendix 1

Beyond Profiling

T he great Greek orator, Demosthenes, was once speaking to a large crowd. The Greeks took their philosophers seriously, and he was speaking on the vital issues of life. He was zeroing in on the things that really mattered, but the throng became disinterested.

Demosthenes was bothered by their lack of attention, so he told a story about a man carrying a bundle of sticks across the desert. The man came upon another man with his donkey. The man with the sticks thought how wonderful it would be if he could hire the other man's donkey to carry his sticks the rest of the way across the desert. It was an interesting story, and the people began to listen again. No one was moving around, and he continued with the story.

The men and donkey eventually stopped to rest in the heat of the day. The man who rented the donkey sat in the shade of the donkey, but the man who owned the donkey protested. He said, "When I rented you the donkey, I did not rent you the shade of the donkey. The shade of the donkey is mine. You'll have to move!"

But the man refused, saying, "When I rented the donkey, I also rented the shade of the donkey." The men argued.

The crowd listened closely to Demosthenes. Just as the people were on the edge of their seats, Demosthenes walked away. The people jeered and clamored for the rest of the story. They demanded an answer to who owned the shade of the donkey. Demosthenes waited till the crowd was very angry, then he returned and rebuked them, "I was speaking to you about the vital issues of life, the things that really mattered, and you paid no attention. Now you demand an answer to the question of who owns the silly shade of an insignificant donkey!"

What a lesson! We can get all wrapped up in the insignificant and silly things of life, but the most important things have eternal values. We often worry about the things that really don't matter. The most significant issues aren't what people do to us. What really matters is how we respond.

Hebrews 12:15 warns us to be careful "lest a root of bitterness spring up to trouble you." The picture is one of cause and effect. The strong emotion of bitterness causes the effect of trouble. There can be serious consequences because of our feelings and actions. Understanding the potential blessings or burdens caused by our responses or reactions is extremely important. People have unique and predictable "hot" and "cold" buttons that determine what they will do under pressure. Personality profiling is not very helpful unless there is some sort of practical application. Discovering one's temperament is only half the benefit of understanding human behavior. We can then apply this information to everyday challenges of life.

The Incredible Hulk Syndrome

When our frustrated feelings push us past the point of normal behavior, we can react to this hurt and become monsters like the fictitious Incredible Hulk. Something happens to us. A startling metamorphosis of emotions and needs change our actions. If we aren't careful, the best thing about us becomes the worst. Our greatest strengths can become weaknesses when we are pushed to extremes. What others once loved most about us, they begin to despise as they observe our overuse and abuse of our strengths. People don't understand what has happened, and they resent the change in our character.

Startling Metamorphosis

Like television's mythical Dr. David Banner, we appear normal one minute and totally different the next, an Incredible Hulk. Something in us snaps when stress stretches us too far. We are transformed into an unusual character that shocks those closest to us.

The Incredible Hulk Syndrome affects people differently. Some people react with outbursts of anger; others totally withdraw. One person throws a fit while another hides. Neither reaction is productive. Most people tend to be either active or passive in their anger. Some go for the jugular while others play dead.

In a family, at work, or in church, our individual responses can be as different as night and day. Frustrations affect our personalities and actions. The effects of stress on our personalities are most evident to those people who are closest to us. Stress spares no one. It touches every area of our lives where we live, work, worship, or play. No matter where we are, we're vulnerable to pressure. Anger is not the only catalyst to our behavior. We may respond in any of a myriad of ways to block our pain and earn some sense of value. If the stress proves too great, our bodies may begin to shut down, and depression may cause us to withdraw into silence and isolation. Our responses to stress are as unique as we are.

Children are also susceptible to this metamorphosis. They become little monsters or throw a pity party and pout for hours. As parents, we need to discover our child's emotional pressure points to avoid their hot buttons and learn to cope with their responses. We may wonder, "How do I deal with this wild child? Why do they act like this when I need them to behave?" And also we ask ourselves, "Why do I respond the way I do? Why do I act like a child at times?" These questions are difficult, but the answers are easier to find than you may think.

Volumes have been written about reversing the problems of uncontrolled emotions, but we may be misunderstanding basic human behavior. The mysterious antidote that cures our behavior is understanding what happens within us and learning to control our feelings rather than letting them control us. Our behavior under pressure is usually very predictable. Our natural responses to pressure are a part of our personalities. We need to control our responses rather than allowing them to control us. Everyone has the potential to turn into a Hulk-like brute or a docile doormat. To better understand what makes us tick, we must understand basic human behavior. By learning more about the technology of temperaments, we can begin to solve the perplexing people puzzle.

Actually, there is more to all this than just becoming personality wise. We can go beyond understanding ourselves; we can know God better. Unfortunately, we can become so interested in human behavior that we neglect knowing the One who made us. Guard against falling into the trap of worshiping the creature more than the Creator.

Meaning In Life

Many people read books like this one hoping to find meaning in life. I hope these pages have been helpful to you, but ultimately, only Christ can provide the meaning, hope, forgiveness, and peace we all need. The concept of a "personal relationship with Christ" may be new to you, or perhaps you've read about it for years. Maybe you are very secure in your relationship with Christ, but my experience shows that many people—even those who attend church regularly—aren't sure if they have accepted Christ as their Savior. You may be at the beginning of your understanding of Christ's love for you, or your may be somewhere on the path of seeking Him. I want to end this book with the most important message I can communicate: how to experience Christ's love, forgiveness, and strength.

If you would like to have a personal relationship with God, first recognize how much you need Him. You may have tried everything and nothing satisfied you (Rom. 3:23.) Without Christ, you have neither hope for heaven when you die nor help here of earth (Rom. 6:23). Christ wants to give you eternal life and abundant life!

Receiving Christ as your Savior is believing He died and rose again so you can know Him personally (John 1:12). You can't work or earn your way into His family (Eph. 2:8,9). All you can do is trust Him the best you know how. You can then know God has forgiven you because He promised He would (1 John 5:13). With Christ in your life, you can allow Him to be Lord of all—including your personality. Jeremiah said it best, "Let not the wise man glory in his wisdom, neither let the mighty man glory in his might, let not the rich man glory in his riches. But let him that glories glory in this, that he understands and knows Me, that I am the LORD," (Jer. 9:23,24). After all is said and done, the only thing that matters is your relationship with Jesus Christ. "I am crucified with Christ, nevertheless I live, yet not I, but Christ lives in me. And the life I now live in the flesh, I live through faith in the Son of God," (Gal. 2:20) Once I understood my relationship to Almighty God—that He loved me, took on flesh, died for me, then rose again to prove it, I no longer had to worry and wonder where I would spend eternity.

I knew for certain I had eternal life because of the finished work of Christ.

The Bible teaches a lot about behavior and motivation. The Apostle Paul challenged believers to be motivated by Christ's love — "For the love of Christ constrains us . . . " (2 Corinthians 5:14). Paul used a unique word, "constrains," to emphasize our appropriate motivation. This word denotes control over something. To constrain our personalities is to control them. Nothing should influence us more than the love of God. The controlling power of the Holy Spirit has made me free to serve God and not self. I know how my personality is influenced by the world, flesh, and the devil. I can now wisely choose to do right rather than wrong—to allow God rather than sin to control my personality.

A Tragic Mistake

Our greatest challenges often come when our spiritual and emotional worlds collide. Learning how to relate to others appropriately is very important. We can solve our people-problems by becoming biblically smart people . To be most effective with people we must honor and obey the One Who made us.

The story is told about a physician who was awakened in the early hours of morning. There had been a terrible automobile accident and a young boy needed emergency brain surgery to save his life. The doctor dressed and drove to the hospital as quickly as possible. He stopped briefly at a red light just to see if any other car was coming. He was about to run the light when a man ran out from behind some bushes. He opened the car door and began yelling at the physician, "Get out! I want your car!" The doctor pleaded, "I'm a doctor . . . ."

But the maniac didn't listen. He screamed again, "Get out or I'm going to kill you!" He then literally dragged the doctor from his car, got in, and sped off.

The physician finally got to the hospital an hour late. The head nurse confronted him, "Where have you been? What took you so long? We've been telling the boy's father you'd be here any minute and that you didn't live far away."

The doctor explained what had happened. The nurse understood, but then she said, "The boy died a few minutes before you arrived. Somebody needs to tell his father. He's really upset because he thinks you didn't hurry enough to get here."

The doctor walked into the waiting room to tell the father his son was dead. There was the man who dragged him out of his car and sped off! Their eyes met in a stunned silence. They both understood the tragedy and the irony of what had happened. The two men could have driven to the hospital together, but the man wouldn't listen.

Under stress, we do crazy things. We don't listen well. We tend to conflict with those who are most important to us. After those times, we may be open to learning more about ourselves and others. The difficulties, then, can have a very positive impact on us and our relationships. We can understand what makes us tick, and what ticks us off.

But must also understand there are more important things in life, than why people do what they do. There are more important things than Human Behavior Science. There are more important things than DISC or even discovering spiritual gifts.

On Beyond Z

On a lighter side, a while back I read some "deep" insights from the great philosopher Dr. Suess entitled, *On Beyond "Z"* or On Beyond Zebra. I don't remember exactly how it went, but tried memorizing it and came out with the following paraphrase:

"Said, Conrad Cornelius O'Donal Odel, my very young friend who was learning to spell, 'A for ape, B is for bear, C is for camel, H is for hair, M is for mouse, R is for rat, and I know all twenty-six letters like that.

Through Z is for Zebra, I know them all well,' said Conrad Cornelius O'Donal Odel.

Then he almost fell flat on his face the floor when I picked up a chalk and drew one letter more. A letter he never dreamed of before.

And I said, 'You can stop with the letter Z. A lot of people stop with a Z, but not me. There are places I go and places I see I could never spell if I stopped with a Z.

I'm telling you this because you're one of my friends. My alphabet starts where your alphabet ends. My alphabet starts with the letter called Uz. It's the letter I use to spell Uzamatuz.

So on beyond Z. Explore like Columbus. Discover new letters like Wum, which is for Wumpish.

My high sounding whale who never comes down until it's time to refill. It's high time you were shown, you really don't know all there is to be known.'"

Dr. Suess has some great insights we should consider. May I add, there are more important letters than DISC. How about considering the letters LORD? Or what about the letters JC or HS for Holy Spirit?

We need to focus on beyond personality profiling and spiritual gifts. We should focus on being filled with the spirit — being controlled by the Holy Spirit, so we don't do what is normal, but what is spiritual. We must focus on the supernatural, rather than the natural.

Then we can best understand what makes us tick, and what ticks us off.

Appendix 2

Warnings!

One of the universal questions of life is, "Why do people do what they do?" The reactions of others—and of ourselves—sometimes surprise and confuse us. The question clamors for an answer, especially among families and faiths. Why do people who live or worship together respond so differently in similar situations?

The answer is simple, yet profound. It's scientific and biblical: We do what we do because of our natural instincts and spiritual motivations. Every person is "wired" with an intricate design of personality and drives from the womb to the grave. This divine design and environmental engineering has made us the way we are. Our motivational pattern should never be an excuse for poor behavior, but it can provide keen insight for understanding why we do what we do.

I want to make it very clear that this study of human behavior from a biblical perspective explains normal, human actions and reactions. Other disciplines recognize abnormal behaviors. Psychologists and psychiatrists have looked at abnormal behavior for decades. I'm not going to deal with the short circuits in brain synapses, chemical imbalances, and psychiatric disorders which cause some people to do crazy things. I'm focusing on the normal everyday problems people have with their feelings, thoughts, and actions.

I don't want anyone to look at the explanations in this book as an excuse for irresponsibility. People in our society spend a lot of time trying to find an excuse for their actions. Every day we hear of someone who blames his past, parents, peers, or pressures for their wrongdoing. There are legitimate cases of abuse and abandonment in which people have reason to blame others, but most of us have overcome our problems and are now responsible adults.

Feelings

One of my greatest concerns deals with feelings. How we respond to our feelings can make or break us. Feelings, in and of themselves, are neither good nor bad. They are just neutral and natural responses to our environment, but the world is full of people who can't cope with their feelings. They use their feelings as excuses for irresponsible behavior.

Feelings are simply the mechanisms that grab our attention. Emotions are the "funny bones" that tell us something just happened. Sometimes we laugh; sometimes we cry; but we definitely respond in some way. We need to learn where these feelings come from in order to control our behavior. What I mean by "where these feelings come from" is the scientific and biblical understanding of our basic human behavior — our natural and supernatural responses to the pressures of life.

I'm not suggesting that all of us need to conduct a deep and difficult exploration into our past that sometimes becomes an excuse for poor behavior. Though I accept the fact that some people suffer today because of their past, many more people use their past as an excuse for irresponsible behavior. Wounds of the past need to be grieved, and the offenses forgiven so we can move on to maturity.

That can be a painful process, but it is necessary if we are to be whole, responsible, loving people.

Responsibility is simply "responding to God's ability" to do right. Responsibility is what makes us behave in a rational way rather than an irrational way.

"Excuse abuse" today has become a national epidemic. Like the common cold, everybody seems to be catching it. We all have problems, disappointments, and struggles in life. We can deal with them in a normal, responsible, and biblical way, or we can choose "fight or flight" in reaction to our unresolved hurt and anger. The choice is up to each of us.

That's Just The Way I Am

Another one of my concerns in identifying our giftedness is when a spouse says, "Well, that's just the way I am. You knew I was like that when you married me. Love me or leave me!" Understanding our motivations and how God made us should never be an excuse for poor behavior. We must live above our feelings and learn to be controlled by the Holy Spirit rather than our emotions.

I know it's not always that simple. Ironically, we define normal as the average, "the norm." There are more people today who come from broken homes and "dysfunctional" backgrounds than ever. The abnormal is nearly the norm today. But most people have learned to deal with their feelings of hurt, misfortune, and abuse. In spite of their past, many of these people have turned into solid citizens and pillars of their churches and communities.

My good friend, Hal Haller, II, shared with me how his son, Hal, III, was preaching at Riverside Baptist Church in Miami. He told me the congregation there included some teenagers who had done some very bad things. One had slashed the pews and pulled out the stuffing during the services. Another had swindled people, giving the church a bad reputation. Still another had hidden alcohol in the boys bathroom and later drank it while playing rock music late at night in the church. Another was sexually active, and even had fist fights with his parents. These kids were "hellions" in the church!

Everyone assumed Hal, as youth minister, was speaking about the current youth of the church, but when he asked these people to stand, they were all adults, leaders in the church. He had been describing their lives years before when they were young and wild! But God had changed their lives: One was the minister of education; another had been a deacon for 20 years; one was studying to be a youth minister; and the last was one of the most excited youth workers in the church.

Hal described working with young people as being like a woman who was pregnant with morning sickness. From the outside everything looks like tough times ahead, but what you don't see is the life stirring within. These people had gone through trying times but had come through it to become mature adults.

Dysfunctional

We'd be surprised to learn how many people had gone through traumatic experiences and yet survived the "abuse excuse" syndrome. Take my life for instance, I just learned that I came from a dysfunctional family. A friend who is a clinical counselor heard my story and concluded my family was truly bizarre!

The problem is I never thought of it as dysfunctional until I was told it was. I have always thought of my years growing up as unfortunate and unusual, but I had choices to make all through my life that would make me "a better or a bitter person." Fortunately, I chose the better way. The only difference between being better or bitter is the letter "I." I also became a Christian at age 13. That was definitely the wisest decision I ever made. It obviously was my salvation, literally and behaviorally. Christ sealed my destiny eternally and emotionally.

I recognize there are many Christians who struggle with their past experiences and present feelings. My answer is simple yet sensitive. We all need to grow up in Christ. We need to mature in our faith in order to handle the trials and troubles of life. I realize there are those who love Jesus, who obey the Scriptures perhaps better than I do, and who may be more faithful to God, but they still suffer. The problem could be chemical imbalance, severe abuse or abandonment, or such grave past offenses that they are scarred for life.

But I'm not a fatalist who accepts these seemingly deterministic factors as prescriptions for doom. I believe God can heal the body, soul, and mind. He can work miracles still today with anyone! Never give up faith in God to heal your broken heart or scarred emotions. God can see you through the toughest of times. I know this may not be easy for you, but perhaps a better understanding of your emotional and spiritual makeup can help. You may also want to seek professional biblical counseling. There are counselors who can help you heal the past. There are also many Christian books available to help you. Perhaps my story in Chapter 2 can also help.

Be careful what you read concerning psychology and human behavior science. Even so-called "Christian psychologists" can give you bad counsel.

Christian Therapists

I agree there are many so-called Christian therapists who have gotten away from the life-changing power of the Scriptures. They tend to spend more time in psychology, rather than the Bible. On the other hand, there are some people who need to spend a little more time understanding their psychological, emotional, and physical makeups. These kinds of counselors may know a lot about the Bible. Some biblical counselors don't recognize the chemical imbalances, psychiatric disorders, or emotional traumas which affect behaviors.

There are many people who genuinely love Jesus and believe the Bible but still have deep psychological problems. These people are like the ones Jesus said "need a physician." Let's not discourage them from the help they so desperately need.

I know of a lady who was a good Christian, active in her church, but who still suffered from depression. She went to her pastor and asked if the elders of the church would anoint her with oil and pray for healing like in the Book of James. The pastor and elders did exactly as the Bible said. They prayed and believed God to heal this sweet woman from her depression. And later, she actually got worse.

She then thought she must have a "demon of depression." This happened at the same time the movie, "The Exorcist," was showing. She was convinced her depression was demonic, so she asked her pastor if he would conduct an exorcism and cast out the demons. He reluctantly cast out the demons, and he thought it worked, but she got even worse. Finally, she went to her gynecologist, began taking estrogen, and got much better. Like this lady, we need to consider all the potential sources of our problems.

I don't mean this to be chauvinistic. Men also have their "male" problems which can be even worse than women. We all have special physical problems from time to time. We shouldn't blame everything on the devil or think every problem is spiritual.

The only problem I ever have with a few counselors and pastors is because they don't accept psychology or human behavior science as truth outside the Bible. They think, "If it isn't in the Bible, it must not be necessary."

Psychobabel

I spoke to a Christian counselor who had criticized my work though he had never seen it. He lumped me with the "psychobabel" crowd. I agree there is a lot of "psychobabel" garbage out there, and I certainly don't believe or teach that psychology is above the Scripture. I always want to sift everything through the grid of Scripture to see if they agree. If not, I always go on the side of the Bible. But if the Bible doesn't discredit science, I feel free to pursue insights through an academic and scientific approach. Remember, science is data which has been amassed, tested, and proven. Science is observable and repeatable.

Hippocrates

The study of human behavior was first developed by Hippocrates 400 years before Christ. He was not an ignorant Greek philosopher. Though pagan in his recognition of "all the gods and goddesses," Hippocrates was a respected physician, the father of modern medicine. He's one of the first who taught us the sanctity of human life, while the real pagans of his day sacrificed babies to their man-made gods. Hippocrates instructed physicians with the "Hippocratic Oath" to protect people from pagan rituals and the so-called science of his day. In his famous oath, he challenged, "I will give no deadly medicine to any one if asked, nor suggest any such counsel; and in like manner I will not give to a woman a pessary to produce abortion." It seems Hippracrates was the first pro-lifer. Those who criticize Hippocrates need to reconsider their stand.

The Pharisees of our day are probably like the skeptics of Hippocrates' era and Christ's day. These pseudo spiritual leaders spout their narrow, rigid versions of truth and drop hyper-biblical bombs on any who dare to disagree. The problem is they don't realize that they are their own worst enemies. They are so narrow they deny the very Scriptures they love.

The Woman At The Well

For example, why did Jesus tell the woman at the well to tell him

about her husband when she asked about living water (John 4)?
She wanted to talk about spiritual things and Jesus insisted she
first talk about her personal, private, and secular life. According to
some "biblical counselors" today, Jesus just failed the test by
confronting her with truth instead of just listening. Jesus knew
what was in her heart and mind. He knew she wasn't ready to deal
with spiritual truth. He had to get her attention and lead her to the
truth. Jesus first dealt with the reality of her heart.

The woman responded to Jesus, "I perceive you are a prophet"
(vs 19). She believed! The woman then went to her city and said,
"Come, see a man who told me all the things I ever did" (vs 28). This
is the same reaction people have to understanding the Four Temperament Model of human behavior when they understand their
motivations more clearly.

There is nothing spooky or psychic about the study of human
behavior. It's like an auto mechanic who can listen to an engine or
connect wires to spark plugs, read some gauges, and tell you exactly
what's right or wrong. Once you're able to discern what makes you
tick, you can often figure out what ticks you off and why you respond
the way you do to the trials and troubles of life. Critics of mixing the
study of human behavior and the Bible don't see the value of God's
revealed truth in nature and God's revealed truth in Scripture. It's
all God's truth, and God should always get all the glory.

Many people are not ready to hear biblical truth, so, like Jesus,
we can use other or scientific truths to grab their attention and
stimulate interest. This approach is like athletes who use their
natural abilities to reach people who would never respond to a
preacher, and entertainers who use their talents to share the
gospel.

On the other hand, the "children of this world are often wiser
than the children of light" (Luke 16:8). Many false religions and
man-made philosophies are reaching multitudes by first touching

heartfelt needs. The cults are experts at taking troubled people and helping their hurts. Many people have used the study of human behavior to promote their false messages. They use a good thing in a bad way.

Human Resources In Ministry

Churches are just now beginning to learn the seriousness of human resources in ministry. Today we hear about networking, assimilating, assessing, and team building in the church more than ever before. Even "reengineering," "demographic studies," and "personality profiling" are being used to improve effectiveness in churches. Understanding motivations and individual giftedness is very important when it comes to changing the style of worship, locations, philosophies of ministry, leadership, staff members, and especially when it comes to building programs,.

Many churches have been nearly destroyed because of ignorance, not so much of spiritual truth, but of people's motivations and abilities. Change is threatening to most people, and they think of their churches as the only secure, stable, and unchanging thing in their lives. Authors Hammer and Champy have written the book, *Reengineering the Corporation*, in which they stress the importance of change, but change can be a disaster if not handled correctly.

Self-Help Phenomena

The self-help and personal development emphasis is quite strong in business and ministry. The world looks for anything and everything to improve the bottom lines — productivity, profit, and the almighty dollar. In contrast, most churches are crippled by fear and ignorance when it comes to human resources and innovation. Instead of being "like a mighty army, moves the church of God," unfortunately we're like a wounded tortoise, treading where we've always trod!

The greatest "growing and going" churches have seen the importance of the study of human behavior in ministry. Instead of being motivated by the almighty dollar, these churches are motivated by almighty God. They are purpose-driven and determined to do a great work for our great God! These churches are on the cutting edge of ministry. They are also the most interested in how Human Behavior Science and human resources can improve their ministries.

Harvard University has one of the best business schools in America. In 1984 Harvard grad, Mark McCormick wrote his best seller, *What They Don't Teach At Harvard Business School*. He entitled chapter one "Reading People!" McCormick claimed that Harvard failed to teach him to understand why people do what they do. He began his book with this subject because he recognized the importance of understanding human behavior in the business world.

Reading people and ministry effectiveness have become priorities in cutting-edge churches. They no longer accept the status quo and old ways of "ministry as usual." Interestingly, the Bible was the first to teach us about the importance of reading people. In 2 Cor. 3:2, Paul tells us, "You are our letter . . . known and read by everybody." The importance of reading people did not come from the business world, but from biblical wisdom. I love the Bible! It is ancient truth for modern times.

Too often, however, the church is not adept at solving its people-problems. In fact, the business world is often better at conflict management than the church. We Christians have the Bible, the Holy Spirit, and all we need to solve our relational problems, but we often fail. While management and labor, government and industry, and even players' unions and owners seem to work out their differences, most churches seem to only split, die, or become the joke of comedians and communities.

Why does the church have such rich resources yet remain so weak in conflict resolution? I seriously believe it's because the church doesn't understand and use the study of human behavior from a biblical perspective. I was speaking in Houston when a man bought my book and asked for my autograph. Someone asked if I knew who the man was? I didn't. So he told me the man was the director of Mission Control at NASA. I discovered he was impressed by what I said during my message.

It is ironic how computer engineers and rocket scientists can communicate with satellites thousands of miles in space, but be unable to communicate with their fellow workers or family members. We can be so successful at high-tech, but fail so miserably at high-touch. Learning how to read people is imperative to success, not because McCormick said so, but because the Bible and science teaches us so.

Psychic Scam

A serious problem often arises when we begin to study human behavior. Sometimes people equate reading people to psychic ability. Some think personality profiling is psychic or like mind-readers! The study of human behavior is not psychic. It's simply the understanding of why people do what they do from a normal and biblical perspective.

I agree we have to be especially careful about those who use so-called science to explain behavior. Astrologers and psychics really concern me. There is nothing scientific about either one. I personally believe the devil counterfeits the truth with these "science." Astrology is a good example of how some people try to explain our behavioral types by the alignment of the stars in the galaxies.

Issac Newton, one of the greatest scientists who ever lived, wrote "Celestial Mechanics" in 1666, in which he disproved astrology. The Bible also condemns astrology in Isa. 47:13. To think the stars can foretell our future when they are controlled by scientific laws set in the heavens is absurd.

I believe psychic predictions are simply random guesses or coincidental happenings. Most psychics are like good gypsies. They learn how to read body language and find little hints along the way. The Public Broadcasting System aired a program in which leading Russian psychics were suppose to be able to describe people from just looking at their photos. The host of the program showed these "world-renowned" psychics the photo of serial killer, Ted Bundy, without their knowledge of his identity. The psychics never mentioned he was a serial killer, nor that he had been dead for several years. They said he was alive, doing well, and a positive person. (Not too close!)

When confronted with the truth about Bundy, the psychics complained that the host did not give them enough information. The host was very careful to not influence the psychics who take information and go on fishing expeditions until they find elements of truth. Like good investigators, they know how to uncover the truth, but unfortunately they always give credit to their so-called psychic powers rather than their intuition and investigative skills.

Gypsy Games

Gypsies are perhaps the most skilled at reading people. They live off gullible people who believe a person's palm or Tarot cards can foretell the future. Gypsies are some of the best con artists and human behavior specialists. They know how to read our eyes, facial expressions, and body language. Gamblers are also experts at reading people. They know "when to fold them and when to hold them" by reading nonverbal communication.

I heard of a horse in England around the turn of the century which, it was claimed, could add and subtract without any human help. No one could figure it out. It was not a trick, and no one helped the horse. It was eventually discovered that the horse had tremendous perception and could detect the slightest hint of approval or disapproval. The horse would tap its hoof on the ground and stop at the correct number when it sensed the approval of people around it. The horse never failed! Then one day, a young girl gave the horse a simple addition problem and the horse failed to answer correctly. Everyone was astonished, then they discovered the girl didn't know the answer either! The horse was looking to her for the approval, but she couldn't give it. Her slightest hint, a gleam in her eyes, or some little expression would have told the horse when to stop tapping, but the girl was clueless. . . and the horse failed. Before that day, some said this horse was psychic, but now you know the truth.

So it is with those who claim to foretell the future or have psychic abilities. There's more fraud and blind faith involved than most people want to admit. It's not scientific, nor biblical, and needs to be avoided. A true and accurate study of human behavior never contradicts the Scriptures, nor does it seek to glorify the flesh or humanity above God.

A Warning!

There is great danger is studying human behavior without a firm commitment to the Bible. If not careful, you can fall prey to one of the greatest lies of all — humanism, the New Age philosophy of life. Humanism tries to deify humans and humanize God. It seeks to make humans into gods and God no greater than humans.

Romans 1:25 warns of the day when we shall "worship and serve the creature more than the Creator." Humanism is actually the lie perpetrated in the Garden of Eden when Satan promised Adam and Eve that they shall be "as gods" (Gen. 3:5). Lucifer tempted Adam and Eve with the same thing that made him fall into sin. Isaiah records that Lucifer wanted to be like god, to sit where God sat, to rule as God ruled, to control his own destiny (Isa. 14:12-14). New Age philosophy today is no different. People everywhere are trying to be gods unto themselves, to be their own gods. Humanism is a false religion and definitely contrary to the Word of God.

There's nothing wrong with trying to improve yourself. Christians ought to be their best at whatever they do. There is tremendous truth in Paul's statement, "I can do all things," but humanism starts with "I" and ends with "things." The Bible starts with God and goes beyond "things" to "Christ." "I can do all things through Christ, who strengthens me" (Phil. 4:13).

Understanding human behavior is like starting at point "A" to get to point "B." To go from point "A" to point "B" you have to start by identifying point "A." It's like getting saved. You have to start by realizing you are lost. Some people can't get saved because they won't accept the fact they are lost. The study of human behavior starts with basic understanding of our condition without Christ. We're sinners in need of a Savior.

Identifying *who* we are is important, but discovering *whose* we are is even more important. Who we are is point "A," and whose we are is point "B." It's a journey with a purpose in mind. We shouldn't study human behavior just to understand why people do what they do. We should study it to learn how to become more like Christ.

Once we trust Christ as our Savior, we need to go on to maturity. We shouldn't just camp at the door of salvation and simply admire the fact that we were once on the other side and now on the inside. We must go on to spiritual growth and development.

Appendix 3

In 1928, William Marston authored *The Emotions of Normal People* in which he introduced the DISC letters to describe the four temperaments. More recently, Dr. John Geier, former Chairman of the Human Behavior Science Department at the University of Minnesota, published the first validated assessment used by business and industry.

Since Dr. Geier's introduction of the Personal Profile System in 1977, many assessments have been developed to identify one's specific personality type. My first *Uniquely You Profiles* were completed in 1993 and have received national attention as a simple and practical instruments. These instruments are self-administering, self-scoring, and self-interpreting.

When you use these profiles, they include everything you need for scoring and interpretation, so there is no waiting and nothing to mail in. You can identify and understand personality types in the convenience of your home, classroom, or office! These profiles are designed to accomplish specific goals, and therefore, are available in a variety of forms.

Uniquely You Resources

- *Discover Your Giftedness 3 Lessons Study Guide*
  Designed specifically for a one day (2 - 3 hours) class. Perfect for new members, leadership, or staff training. Features personality, spiritual gifts, talents, and interests profiles. Teacher's Manual available.

• *Discover Your Giftedness 6 - 13 Weeks*
Study Guide
Designed specifically for a 6 - 13 weeks Sunday School curriculum, Sunday afternoon or evening church training, home or mid-
week Bible study curriculum. Perfect for new members, leadership, and / or staff training. Features personality, spiritual gifts,
talents, and interests profiles. Teacher's Manual available.

Both *Discover Your Giftedness Study Guides* combine 9 Spiritual
Gifts and 4 Personalities; Feature 36 Blends of Spiritual Gifts
and Personality Types, How To Handle Conflicts, and Opportunities For Ministry.

• *Uniquely You Combination Profile* (Biblical)
Featuring 7 Spiritual Gifts and 4 Temperaments, Discovering
and Controlling Your Behavioral Blends, Leadership Insights,
Involvement Insights, Conflict Resolution, and Opportunities
For Ministry.

• *Uniquely You Personality Profile* (Standard)
Featuring Discovering Your Behavioral Blends, Leadership In-
sights, Practical Application, Intensity Insights, How To Handle
Conflicts, and Challenging Differences.

• *How To Control & Conquer Feelings*
Featuring the Child's and Parent's Profile with 2 questionnaires,
For ages 4-12 and their parents, Featuring Two Graphs: "This is
expected of me" and "This is me," Child / Parent Reflections,
Motivating & Disciplining Child, Parenting Styles.
        Kit with Guidebook and 90 minute Audio Cassette with
Instructions, Interpretation and Application available,
(Biblical)

- *Uniquely You Multi-Purpose* (Biblical)
  Featuring Involvement Insights, Conflict Resolution, Relation-
  ships Insights, Dynamic Differences, Dating / Singles Insights,
  Outreach & Discipleship Insights, Teaching Insights.

- *Relationships Profile* with 2 questionnaires (Biblical)
  Featuring Intensity Indexes, Opposites Attract and Attack,
  plus Relationship Reflections. Teacher's Manual available.

- *Professional's Profile* (Standard)
  Featuring Interviewing / Hiring Insights, Selling and Servic-
  ing, Selling Styles, Buying Styles, Dealing with Objections,
  First Signs, and Recruiting Customers.

- *Men's Profile* (Biblical)
  Used by Promise Keepers. Great for men's small group Bible
  studies and leadership training. Teacher's Manual available.

- *Wellness Dynamics Profile* (Standard)
  Improving your health, happiness, and business opportunity.
  Focusing on how personalities respond to diet, exercise, and
  food supplements, along with being a better business builder.

- *Woman's Profile* (Biblical)
  Great for personal development, women's conferences, Bible
  studies, and counseling.

- *The Adventures of You & Me-Z in the
  Land of Feelings* (Standard)
  For Ages 6 - 12; Featuring 30 minute audio cassette Musical
  Drama and Coloring Book for children to understand why they
  do what they do and how to control their feelings.

• *Manuals & Audio Cassettes Kit* (Biblical or Standard)
  Understanding Human Behavior Science from biblical and
  business perspectives.

To order these resources, call or write to
Uniquely You Ministries
    P. O. Box 490
    Blue Ridge, GA 30513
    Information Phone: (706) 632-8411
    Order Phone: (800) 501-0490
    Fax: (706) 632-3484

Certification Training

If you are interested in Certification Training, be sure to contact Uniquely You Ministries. This training can expand your professional and personal goals, and equip you to help others live, work, and relate to others more effectively.

One Day Certification Training

THE BIGGEST MISTAKE LEADERS MAKE
Managing everyone the same way!
- What the scientific studies reveal about Human Behavior Science.
- Balancing High-Tech with High-Touch needs.
- Understanding the Four Temperament Model of Human Behavior.

SOLVING THE MYSTERY OF MOTIVATION
Understanding everyone is already motivated!
- Simplifying leadership . . . Practical application.
- What makes people tick (finding their "hot & cold buttons.")
- Understanding there are no bad personalities.
- Developing leadership through flexibility.
- Evangelism & Discipleship according to temperament types.

OVER USING YOUR STRENGTHS BECOMES ABUSIVE
Guarding the best and avoiding the worst thing about you!
- How to deal with stress and pressure.
- Leading people according to their temperaments.
- Speaking and teaching to the interests/needs of everyone.
- Adapting teaching styles to specific learning styles.

REDUCING CONFLICTS /
INCREASING INVOLVEMENT
Networking Without Conflict Management Is Disastrous!
- Policies and Procedures on "How To Handle Conflicts"
- A proven Resolution Management Covenant.
- What to do when you see trouble brewing.
- Instilling loyalty and faithfulness.

TEAM BUILDING
Identifying and Understanding Group Dynamics!
- How to build a *Team* atmosphere.
- Surrounding yourself with the right people.
- How each person *fits* to make the team most effective.
- Improving Team Building through personality profiling.
- Interviewing prospective employees more effectively.
- Helpful hints in selecting staff and leadership based upon spiritual gifts and personality types.
- Ways to avoid problems before completing hiring process.
- Determining the strengths and weaknesses of a group without being threatening.
- Designing strategies to balance the effectiveness of a group.
- Using computers for personnel prospecting.

PREPARING YOUR MINISTRY FOR GROWTH
Creating an atmosphere and environment for growth!
- Assessing and profiling the ministry's specific needs.
- Identifying specific elements for growth.
- Hidden pitfalls of growing organizations.
- Changing tradition without creating division.

IMPLEMENTING PROVEN ASSIMILATION PROGRAM
How To Conduct 2 or 3 Hour; or 3, 6, & 13 Weeks Classes!
- Step-by-step how to promote and conduct classes.
- Create momentum and enthusiasm without hype.
- When, Who, and Why to conduct New Member Classes.
- Place members in ministries based upon their giftedness.
- Avoiding the too expensive and little results programs.
- Review of other assimilation / *networking* programs.
- Develop **Leadership Team** to do *"work of the ministry."*

MARKETPLACE EVANGELISM
How to develop seminars to reach business people!
- Taking advantage of the *yuppie* self-help phenomena!
- Innovative outreach ideas that work.
- New strategies to reach today's family.
- How *trends* may be affecting your ministry.
- Specific reason for declining effectiveness.
- *Improve Your People Fitness* Seminar.

CHANGE MANAGEMENT
Reengineering and / or Retooling The Church?
- Redefining reengineering and change management.
- Understanding the why and need for reengineering.
- Avoiding the *"seeds of destruction"* as you reengineer.
- Developing strategies to assure reengineering success.
- Discovering hidden factors that can destroy results.
- Communicating reengineering more effectively.

Three Days Advanced Certification Training
Training Trainers To Conduct Seminars and Do Consulting

Topics include:

WHAT TO DO AND *NOT* TO DO IN STARTING-UP
Getting started without going broke!
- Two definite "don'ts" to avoid the first week of your new venture.
- Balancing "High I" enthusiasm with "High C" wisdom.
- Why certain personality types tend to succeed or fail in starting up.
- How every personality can build a great training business / ministry.
- Developing a plan and blue print for success.

MARKETING YOUR MINISTRY AND / OR BUSINESS
Dealing with the most difficult challenge of all!
- Four sure ways to increase your responses.
- Getting strangers to invite you to conduct training.
- Avoiding the "friends and relatives discouragements."
- One proven equation that works in getting seminars.
- Getting seminars without writing letters or making   phone calls.

BUSINESS SENSE IN STARTING YOUR MINISTRY
Important practical advise no one ever told me!
- Starting a nonprofit versus a for-profit business / ministry.
- Getting a credit card merchant's account to process cards.
- How to earn free airline tickets and cutting your transportation costs.

- Establishing fees for speaking and training services.
- Self-publishing and developing your own resources for added sales.

IN-DEPTH INTERPRETATION OF DISC GRAPHS
Reading people and their profile graphs like a road map!
- Understanding the differences in Graphs 1 & 2.
- Describing Behavioral Blends in positive, but constructive ways.
- Dealing with the difficult explanations.

USING PROFILES FOR DIFFERENT PURPOSES
Expanding your potential and profit by diversifying your use of profiles!
- Using Relationships Profile for Counseling and Marriage Conferences.
- How Men's and Woman's Profiles can open doors of opportunities.
- Innovative use of the Child's / Parent's Profile for outreach.
- Using the Professional's Profile to conduct training for businesses.
- Which profile every church should use.
- How to use each profile most effectively.
- Getting churches and businesses to order resources from you.

COMPARING "NETWORKING" ASSESSMENTS
Reviewing various assessments and networking resources!
- Understanding the "pros" and "cons" of the most popular profiles.
- Evaluating the costs versus results of using various profiles.
- Recognizing the most common mistake in most profiles today.
- Why personality types and spiritual gifts should be taught

together.
- Understanding the importance of not using too many spiritual gifts.
- Why the DISC model is often better than Myers-Briggs.
- Identifying over 20 different models of Human Behavior Science.
- A bibliography to die for / A must for every personal library.

Corporate Training
"Improve Your People Skills"
For Businesses, Organizations and Individuals

Dr. Mels Carbonell and / or one of his associates are available for seminars, workshops, retreats/conferences, Keynote banquet speaker, consulting and any Human Behavior Science need. They also conduct training in Team Building, Effective Selling, Customer Satisfaction, Hiring, Stress & Conflict Management.

Training can be customized to fit any schedule from 30 minutes to on going training. His most popular formats are Basic / Advanced Training (full day / 6 hours) and Basic Training only (half day / 3 hours).

THE BIGGEST MISTAKE LEADERS MAKE
Managing everyone the same way!
• What the most recent scientific studies reveal about behavior.
• How to read people like a book.
• Balancing High-Tech with High-Touch.
• Understanding the Four Temperament Model of Behavior.

SOLVING THE MYSTERY OF MOTIVATION
Understanding everyone is motivated!
• Discovering why people do what they do.
• Simplifying leadership . . . Practical application.
• Identifying what mainly motivates you and others.
• Understanding there are no bad personalities.
• Developing leadership through flexibility.

PREDICTING RESPONSES / AVOIDING CONFLICTS
Why intimidation and manipulation don't work!
• How to lead and be led most effectively.
• How each personality responds in conflict.
• Discovering what makes you tick & what ticks you off.
• Designing Resolution Management policies and procedures.
• Hidden pitfalls of growing organizations.

HANDLING AND CHANGING POOR ATTITUDES
Creating an atmosphere and environment for success!
• How to deal with stress and pressure.
• The Incredible Hulk Syndrome.
• Turning soar grapes into sweet employees.
• Identifying which of 21 Behavioral Blends best describes you.

OVER USING STRENGTHS BECOMES ABUSES
Guarding the best and avoiding the worst thing about you!
• Why and how opposites attract and attack.
• How to get more done with less time / resources.
• Discerning your's and other's "hot buttons."
• Speaking and teaching to the interests and needs of others.

CHANGE MANAGEMENT
"Reengineering The Corporation" Results!
• Redefining reengineering and change management.
• Understanding the why and need for reengineering.
• Avoiding the "seeds of destruction" as you reengineer.
• Developing strategies to assure reengineering success.
• Discovering hidden factors that can destroy results.
• Appealing to four basic temperament types to communicate reengineering more effectively.

TEAM BUILDING
Understanding Why The Biggest Problem In
Business Is Not Technical — It's Relational!

- How to build a "Team" atmosphere.
- Guarding against surrounding yourself with people just like you.
- How each person "fits" to make the team most effective.
- Improving Team Building through personality profiling.
- Solving employee problems before you hire.
- Interviewing prospective employees more effectively.

SELLING AND SERVICING
How "People Based" Selling and Servicing Works!

- When and how to sell and service according to personalities.
- How to read "body language" to improve presentation and / or sales approach.
- Dealing with objections to redirect results.
- How to close the sale more effectively by understanding customers motivations.
- How to get customers coming back and grow your business without a lot of hype.

For more information about these seminars, write or call:
Leadership Institute of America
  P. O. Box 490
  Blue Ridge, GA 30513
  Information Phone: (706) 632-8411
  Order Phone: (800) 501-0490
  Fax: (706) 632-3484

Computer Generated Reports

Human Behavior Resources have become extremely effective and essential in management and leadership. Many individuals, companies, churches, and schools now use computer generated personality profiles to help counsel individuals, interview prospective staff, develop leadership, assess students or teachers, and resolve member or employee conflicts.

All reports (except *Personal Analysis*) can be generated on PC or Mac computers. There is no extra software to purchase or install. You can have an individual complete his or her questionnaire; then you enter the results into the computer within minutes and, print a profile. It's so easy and comprehensive you will never want to counsel or hire anyone without it.

Personal Analysis Computer Report

The Uniquely You C•A•N Personal Analysis Report is for churches to identify members' natural and spiritual giftedness. The program's purpose is networking members into ministry for more effective results.

This *"first-of-its kind"* program features four reports in one — ***The Spiritual Gifts Profile, Personality Profile, Talents / Interests Survey, and Biographical Information.***

The *Spiritual Gifts Profile* identifies nine motivational gifts — *Prophecy, Teaching, Service, Exhortation, Administration, Giving, Showing Mercy, Evangelism, and Pastor / Shepherd*. This Profile interprets and applies the results of a person's Spiritual Gifts.

The *Personality Profile* identifies the four basic temperaments with specific letters *(D, I, S and C)*, in relation to the Greek titles *(Choleric, Sanguine, Phlegmatic and Melancholy)*. The profile also identifies 21 Behavioral Blends or composites of DISC behavior.

Once a person's Spiritual Gift/s, Personality Types, Talents, and Interests are identified, practical steps of action are presented to answer — *'What Now?'* Each Report concludes with suggested opportunities for ministry. You get unlimited reports, but each new person costs $3 - $5.

A *"Biblical Resolution Management"* Covenant also helps avoid and resolve conflicts. This Covenant encourages members to follow Matthew 18 *("go to the brother first alone")* and 1 Timothy 5:19 *("rebuke not an Elder")*. It gives step-by-step instructions on how to deal with personnel and volunteer clashes.

Churches are hindered most because of *"people problems."* The more involved in ministries, the more potential for conflicts. Many churches are attempting to develop networking programs, but assimilation without teaching resolution management leads to ultimate division.

Uniquely You C•A•N Personal Analysis is designed to solve *"people problems"* — to deal with your church's greatest needs. The *"bottom line"* of the program is **RESULTS!** Improving relationships, handling conflicts, increasing involvement, and stimulating church growth is what Uniquely You is all about.

MANAGING FOR SUCCESS
Three Different Versions To Choose —
1) Employee / Manager;   2) Team Building;   3) Sales

These reports are generated from each self-contained computer disk. Each report is saved on the disk. You can rerun any individual's report as many times as needed. It only costs to enter each new person on to the disk.Companies often pay hundreds of dollars for these types of reports.

You can now get cutting-edge insights for the fraction of the cost of what businesses would pay.

Each E/M Report Contains:

- *General Characteristics*
- *Value To The Organization*
- *Checklist for Communicating*
- *Don'ts On Communicating*
- *Communication Tips*
- *Ideal Environment*
- *Perceptions*
- *Descriptors*

- *Natural and Adapted Style*
- *Keys To Motivating*
- *Keys To Managing*
- *Areas For Improvement*
- *Behavioral Factor Indicator*
- *DISC Graphs*
- *Action Plan*

Relationships Insights

Perfect For

- Marriage Counseling • Marriage Enrichment
- Pre-marital Counseling • Personal Development

These reports are designed specifically for the busy pastor and / or counselor who needs a quick, but accurate diagnostic, simple to use and understand tool, plus inexpensive insights for more effective counselling.

Includes:

General Statements
- *Current Wants*
- *Relationship Strengths*
- *Keys To Communication*

- *Barriers To Communication*
- *Hindering Factors*
- *DISC Graphs*
- *Personalized Action Plan*

Successful Career Planning

These reports are perfect for individuals looking for help in choosing a career. It uses the DISC Model of Human Behavior, plus two other questionnaires to give advise as to which careers might fit them best.

Includes:

Personal Characteristics
- *Personal Strengths*
- *Basic Needs*
- *Response To The Environment*
- *Present Wants*
- *Idea Environment*
- *Checklist For Communicating*
- *Strengths & Weaknesses*

CAREER JOB ANALYSIS
- *Drive - Challenge*
- *Influencing - Contacts*
- *Steadiness - Consistency*
- *Compliance - Constraints*

JOB INDICATOR
- *Listing of Suggested Occupational Types*

For more information about our computer reports, write or call:
Leadership Institute of America
 P. O. Box 490
 Blue Ridge, GA 30513
 Information Phone: (706) 632-8411
 Order Phone: (800) 501-0490
 Fax: (706) 632-3484

Order
What Makes You Ticks

Only
$9.95
Retail: $14.95

282 Pages

I want to order ___ (quantity) of the new *What Makes You Tick* book
for $9.95 each, plus $3.95 shipping.

Your Name _____Phone (_____) _____

Address (Indicate Church or Home) _____

City_____ State _____ Zip _____

Uniquely You™ *Resources* • P. O. Box 490 • Blue Ridge, GA • 30513
Order phone: (800) 501-0490 • Info. phone: (706) 632-8411 • Fax: (706) 632-3484